The Gift c
Iona Pilgrim Ways

The Gift of Stillness
Iona Pilgrim Ways

Rosemary Power

 www.**iona**books.com

Copyright © Rosemary Power 2024

First published 2024 by
Wild Goose Publications
Suite 9, Fairfield
1048 Govan Road, Glasgow G51 4XS, Scotland
A division of Iona Community Trading CIC
Limited Company Reg. No. SC156678
www.ionabooks.com

ISBN 978-1-80432-314-4

Cover photo © David Coleman

The publishers gratefully acknowledge the support of the Drummond Trust, 3 Pitt Terrace, Stirling FK8 2EY in producing this book.

All rights reserved. Apart from the circumstances described below relating to non-commercial use, no part of this publication may be reproduced in any form or by any means, including photocopying or any information storage or retrieval system, without written permission from the publisher via PLSclear.com.

Non-commercial use:
The material in this book may be used non-commercially for worship and group work without written permission from the publisher. If photocopies of sections are made, please make full acknowledgement of the source, and report usage to CLA or other copyright organisation.

Rosemary Power has asserted her right in accordance with the Copyright, Designs and Patents Act, 1988, to be identified as the author of this work.

Overseas distribution
Australia: Willow Connection Pty Ltd, 1/13 Kell Mather Drive, Lennox Head NSW 2478
New Zealand: Pleroma, Higginson Street, Otane 4170, Central Hawkes Bay

Printed in the UK by Page Bros (Norwich) Ltd

CONTENTS

Acknowledgements 7
Introduction 8
Part one – places of prayer 15
Following the carved Word: Columban and medieval 15

Saint Martin's Cross 17
Reilig Odhràin (Oran) 29
Iona nunnery 36
The cow in the crossing 46
For understanding among the nations 53

The Word through others: Iona prayers from recent times 59

Deep peace of the running wave 60
Prayer for our own reshaping 67
The Master Carpenter 71
I bind unto myself today 79
The Ravensbrück prayer 89

Part two – a cloister pilgrimage 93

The east side 98
The south side 108
The west side 115
The north side 123

Part three – pilgrimage by boat 131

1. The jetty 133
2. Martyrs' Bay 136
3. Along the coast 139

4. Sandeels Bay   139
5. The marble quarry   142
6. Columba's Bay   145
7. The Boiling Pot   150
8. Bay at the Back of the Ocean   150
9. The machair   151
10. Along the coast   153
11. The north coast   155
12. White Strand of the Monks   158
13. Towards the abbey   161
14. Heading southwards   163
15. The nunnery and the return   164
16. Back to the jetty   166

Afterword   167

Sources   171

Further reading   174

ACKNOWLEDGEMENTS

Very many people have helped with the preparation of this book. Most of the photographs are courtesy of David Coleman, who made many useful suggestions on the text. Some poems and prayers have appeared in *Coracle* and other Iona Community publications, while several of the reflections first appeared in shorter form in the Iona Community's Prayer Circle Newsletter when I was the Co-ordinator. I am grateful for comments made by Members of the Iona Community, especially in the Highland region. Tony Phelan read over the text and made crucial suggestions. The Benedictine Community at Kylemore Abbey in Connemara, Ireland, showed me the liturgical rhythm of their tradition and the places of silence. Emily Wilkins of the National Trust for Scotland and Mull & Iona Community Trust provided information. Kathy McVittie gave her botanical expertise to the modern carvings on the cloister arches, Joyce Watson commented on the prevalence of the flowers and birds on Iona, and Molly Harvey gave background to the sponsorship of the carvings. Davy Kirkpatrick lent his expertise as an islander and a fisherman to the boat pilgrimage. Gilbert Márkus allowed the use of his translation of *Noli Pater*; and the family of Margaret Connor (1929–2014) gave permission to use some of her poems. Finally, my thanks are due to all those who visited Iona over the last thirty years who attended events I ran there, then gave freely of their knowledge and understanding, all of which has helped in the creation of this book. Any errors are my own. This book is dedicated to the memory of my brother Keith Power (1960–2018).

INTRODUCTION

Spending time on Iona can give us a new sense of who we are because, for many, we are given time to meet God. We give expression to this experience through what we have received and want to take with us, and through what we leave behind. Iona constantly receives blessing from the people who visit, and this augments the blessing already in this place where prayer has been practised for so long. Some people are aware of being touched in their depths, while others, especially those who come curiously as tourists, may find something more that draws them to return.

Pilgrimage involves a spiritual journey, often exacting, to a place of special significance, the time spent there, and the returning. It may be undertaken alone or with companions, and may involve the desire to unite with the experience of others in the past as well as in the present. This book is essentially for pilgrims, especially for those who want to slow down, either because they wish to, or because physical limitation means they have to, but who can equally take the inner journey further without movement of the body.

The writing is based on both personal reflection, expressed mainly through poetry, and historical research on Iona in past times and present, with the intention that it may be of use to those who journey to the island as pilgrims. It is hoped that the contents are of interest to all who come, but the focus is on the gift of staying still, to allow an image or a scene, or words, to open to the listener or viewer. They are also, on a practical level, selected with regard to their accessibility for those who cannot undertake much physical exercise.

The book therefore tries to work on two levels. On one it seeks to help with the interpretation of some of the carvings and buildings of Iona, the prayers that have been associated with the island, and the places visited by the pilgrimages around the island that are important to many people. There have been many fantastical versions of Iona the Holy Isle, and these can be important as starting points on a journey, or ways to respect what others seek to find here. But the history and archaeology of the island and its monuments can put us in touch with our predecessors, and to some people, especially those who come frequently, knowledge about the past is an aid to deepening spiritual reflection. The way people have thought and acted in the past can help us explore the present.

The other level is for those who wish to ignore much detail, and concentrate on specific sites, carvings or prayers.

The first section of reflections can be undertaken alone and at the individual's own pace. The abbey buildings are Benedictine, and like the nunnery were designed for the monastic round of private and public prayer, work and recreation, all in the same place, in accordance with the Order's commitment to stability. The Benedictine tradition of *lectio divina*, 'sacred reading', is taken here, the slow, individual repetition of a short piece of scripture until it becomes part of the heart, and occupies enough of the mind to allow the spirit to enjoy time silently with God. We have here visual prompts in the stonework, and for more recent times prayers that are associated with Iona.

The second part, the 'pilgrimage' around the cloisters, can be done alone or with a handful of others, and focusses on the inner stillness that can be assisted by art, by looking for a time at a created piece of work and allowing it to open its inner meaning to the viewer. It is again suited to *lectio divina* in the context of reflection on modern carving; and can be broken off and completed at a later date, or even off the island, using photographs of the carvings.

One of the major activities for pilgrims on Iona had been the weekly pilgrimage round the island, organised by staff of the Iona Community. But many, including myself, have been physically unable to undertake these journeys. The final pilgrimage is therefore by boat, and involves the movement and sound of the sea, the capacity to look, and enjoy what others have experienced before us, in this part of God's creation. It covers nearly all the stopping-places visited by the walkers, and a few more as well. As chartering a local boat is usually a group activity, this section is designed for pilgrimage with others, and may be an opportunity for the long-standing practice of sharing stories and songs on the way.

This book is dedicated to the memory of the health workers who lost their lives at the time of its writing, during the Covid-19 pandemic. The United Kingdom and Ireland saw high death rates but the suffering was overall much less than in countries with weaker health and transport systems. The pandemic links us to the past: Columba's monks suffered several outbreaks of 'plague', including one in 664, the year of the Northumbrian Synod of Whitby. Then in 683 came a plague that particularly affected children, while a three-year plague around the year 700 led to widespread famine. Later, in the fourteenth century, the Black Death dramatically cut the population of all Europe by perhaps a third. The people of the past knew that their communities could be wiped out by these epidemics, the more so if they cared for the sick, which meant that far from being 'self-isolating' they were in the thick of the illness and likely to catch it themselves.

The people of Iona, and elsewhere, were risking not only their lives but a way of life in their following Christ into danger. The pandemic hit us at a time of great threat to the environment, when the climate crisis indicated uncontrollable change to the planet, with parts of it becoming uninhabitable, in consequence causing vast movements of people seeking scarcer resources. The people of Iona would have had similar fears, whether the harvest was poor for two or more years running, or during the centuries of Viking raids that tore people from their homes and brought in turn new settlers to the islands. Again, we can link our prayers to those of the past in this place.

Many wondered whether the pandemic would finally bring the death of the institutional churches, and what would be lost as well as how the vital elements would be expressed in future. Christians seek to enter the cloud of unknowing that is God's will, in a willingness to seek new ways of proclaiming the Gospel. For those within church life there must be a question of whether what is dear, or at least familiar, may need to die, and whether it can do it triumphantly, with the heritage passed on to new life. The monastic communities of Iona knew change, in seeking to rebuild after the Viking destructions; and later coping with changes to church organisation and liturgy that led to Columba's island adopting Benedictine and Augustinian Rules and the buildings that go with these changes.

The early Christian and medieval community on Iona knew the cost in suffering and love; and their prayers as people died without the pain relief and medical care the Western world takes for granted may be part of their contribution to the deeply spiritual atmosphere of Iona today, an atmosphere that contains strength and the capacity to absorb suffering while giving back love. The island's story touches our present concerns while it informs our knowledge of this place. The island is where many find a spark of the Divine, the endlessly practical and inexplicable gift of love which expands as the need arises, and allows those on earth to find heaven drawn down to meet them.

Iona remains a place of pilgrimage, a place where people meet a love large enough to hold their questioning and grief and bring away with them strange gifts of love and blessing.

A note on spelling:

The spelling of Old Irish, the common literary language of both Ireland and Gaelic Scotland in the Columban monastic period, changed over time. I have used the most familiar form of personal names.

While modern Irish retains the use of the acute accent (´) to mark lengthened vowels, modern Scots Gaelic uses the grave accent (`), and this has been used for the place-names of Iona.

Prayer before writing

Christ, net-maker and mender,
who wrote letters in the sand,
on the palm of your hand,

be with us as we seek
to be tools that weave
and link the words,
to hold your plans,
to let in light
of meanings you would net
in unknown places.

And so, before we start,
we offer you, though piecemeal, lives and time,
the fears, the doubts, the skills, the stress,
and our experience.

Be you the guide and worker:
that your gifts be the means
by which our labour's caught
in other hearts,
to feed your world your Word.

Rosemary Power

PART ONE – PLACES OF PRAYER

Following the carved Word:
Columban and medieval

O Columba, Spes Scotorum

Mouth for the speechless
light for the blind
feet for the fallen –
stretch out your hand

strengthen the silenced
and suffering in mind.

So, Columba, hope of Scotland,
and of Ireland,
and of all lands,
by your merits' mediation
and angelic intervention
help us pilgrims on this journey.

Based on 'Columba, Spes Scotorum, Hope of Scots', from the medieval Inchcolm Antiphonary

SAINT MARTIN'S CROSS

This photograph of Saint Martin's Cross, the narrow ring-headed cross that stands just west of Iona Abbey, was taken after the rain.

The monastery Saint Columba had founded was about three centuries old when this cross was erected; so fifteen to twenty generations of monks, pilgrims and islanders had already prayed and worked here. Then, not long before its raising, old certainties about what church life was and what place it held in society had been shattered by the arrival of Vikings. They knew nothing of these certainties or the faith that had given birth to them, but came to plunder and enslave. They raided first in 795, burnt Iona in 802, and killed 68 of the community in 806. In 825 they returned with an interpreter, and one monk was killed brutally when he refused to say where the monastery's precious relics were hidden. His martyrdom was commemorated in verse composed in what is now Switzerland, and was recounted across Europe.

So, in these times of turbulence this cross was raised, carved with scenes from the scriptures on one side and on the other with a pattern of snakes moving upwards. With so much of what had been cherished now looted or burnt, with the young men killed or captured, the community brought a single large piece of stone from Mull, and raised this cross. Perhaps it occurred at around the year 815, when the abbot and many of the community departed to Kells with many of the portable treasures.

Was it a way to proclaim the permanence of their faith, in good times and terror times, and their desire that this faith should be seen? Is this a starting place for personal pilgrimage, through light and shadow, dawn, daylight and darkness?

It was not the only high cross on Iona but is the only one that has never fallen or been taken down. In the earlier days of the monastery wooden crosses had been raised, at marking points on paths, and at the entrances to the monastic site. Gravestones too had crosses etched on them, some of them a ring-head, and some with interlace decorations. Of the freestanding stone crosses, the two oldest fell and broke but are now both raised again under cover of the museum. They are the Saint John's Cross, a replica of which stands in the original base outside Saint Columba's

Chapel, and the Saint Odhràin Cross. A later cross, of which the shaft and part of the ring-head survives, is the Saint Matthew's Cross. This is now also under cover, though its original base still stands where it was raised, to the west of the Abbey Church.

The names we use for the crosses may go back to these times, though it can't be proved. A Welsh scholar, Edward Lhuyd (1660-1709), who visited Iona in the 1690s, first writes that this cross was named after Martin, the fifth-century soldier turned monk, who became the model for Western monastic life, and after whose written *Life* Adomnán modelled his *Life of Saint Columba*. This text is the source of most of what we know of Iona's most famous saint.

We are learning to understand the crosses again, with their artistic similarities to the work of silversmiths of the early Christian period, and what they meant to those who raised them, and why they were placed where they were. One of our artistic sources is the decorated manuscript of the Gospels the Book of Kells, which was very probably compiled on Iona along with many other manuscripts.

The carvings make use of international symbols, and the east side of this cross caught the morning sun, providing us with the first meditation.

The snakes refer to the redeemed Christian who sloughs off sin like last year's skin and starts again. The snakes are entwined: we do this in community with others, and through community rise upwards towards God. Jesus said that he would be raised up as Moses lifted the bronze snake of healing in the desert, and that all people would be drawn to him (John 3:13–15, 8:28, 12:32, based on Numbers 21:4–9). A serpent on a staff is the international sign for healing, for medical treatment. The Gospels call us to be as wise as serpents as well as innocent as doves.

The lone serpent of Eden presents wisdom and prudence distorted to verbal venom. This image is not found on Saint Martin's Cross, but is depicted together with Adam and Eve on the east shaft of the Saint Matthew's Cross, which stood nearby. Before the Benedictine church was built in the early thirteenth century, this carving caught the sun as did the life-affirming snakes of Saint Martin's Cross, one reminding the monks each day of the start of the story of sin and toil, and the other of redemption and community.

The involvement of many people working together is evident when we explore how this cross was made. The carving is without apparent slips in the rough granite. The east face is blank in its lower reaches, and then shows the snakes curled around each other and around protruding bosses. Although the cross is carved from a single piece of stone, the design on this face shows a break, which gives the upper parts into the dimensions of a Coptic cross, which appears as if raised on the shaft. But it may have had another profile too, for the short arms have slots in their ends, and there is one also in the head, and these may have been used to add wooden extensions to form the more normal proportions for a high cross. Alternatively, they may have been used to insert short metal and gemstone ends to form a *crux gemmata*, a jewelled, shining cross, to be seen from afar. The bosses, which look as if they were modelled on the fine metalwork produced on Iona at the time when the cross was raised, may also have held in their empty centres worked and gilded silver.

The *crux gemmata* is the subject of the Old English poem *The Dream of the Rood*, in which the shining cross itself speaks to the dreaming poet, telling the story of Christ's crucifixion from its own perspective. Relationships are between the physical and the mystical, the scriptural cross of redemption and the significance in the world for all time, and includes the part we play in the story. Part of the poem was carved in runic script onto the freestanding high cross raised at Ruthwell, on the south-west coast of what is now Scotland.

Saint Martin's Cross was not only to be viewed but to be engaged with in prayer, and the uncarved lower part might show us how this could be done physically, though if it was done it has left no mark in wearage on the stone. The cross stands in its original base, carved with three steps, which recall the tradition of three falls of Jesus when carrying the cross; and there is a small area of this base at ground level which juts out. Kneeling upon this the pilgrim could put their head against the uncarved section of this east face, in doing so joining with Jesus on his journey through pain to death. This means uniting too with the community of believers on that same journey, who are represented in the intertwined snakes that move upwards towards the central boss, which perhaps once glowed silver in the morning sun, a reminder of the first morning of the Resurrection.

The sides of this cross are not carved at all, unlike many other crosses. There is a ring-head, which was not always the case with all high crosses: on the older Saint Odhràin's Cross a ring-head is implied through the carved-away 'armpits', while Saint John's Cross, which is also older, had both 'armpits', and a ring-head added later to better bear the weight of the arms. The ring-head so closely associated with the high crosses contains rich layers of imagery. The design comes in part from the south of Europe and late classical sculpture where the image of the cross of Christ bears the laurel wreath of victory rather than the crown of thorns.

This is combined with an artistic device found in some ancient manuscripts. In these, the first letter of the Chi-Rho, the Greek 'Χρι' (the monogram of Christ's name), has the 'X' turned to form an upright cross, while the Greek 'R', which is written as 'P', has the round part of the letter centralised and made to encircle it, while the stem and the final 'I' are both incorporated into the upright of the turned 'X', the three together forming a ring-headed cross. As with any powerful symbol, the ring-head is an indicator with no fixed 'meaning', and many have found other ways to interpret it since, in terms of the sun and the seasons.

The biblical figures on the west face of Saint Martin's Cross attract most attention, and can be a source of meditation for us as it was for our ancestors. They are best read from the bottom upwards.

The four figures in the lowest band of imagery are the least easy to interpret. To the left, as we face the cross, we see a figure with hands perhaps joined, and then a taller one with the right arm raised. Beside is another upright figure, possibly wearing priestly robes, the head slightly inclined towards the one on the far right, and an arm possibly outstretched towards that figure's arm or knee. This last figure is sitting, or perhaps kneeling. Is this one scene or two? Is the person with the upright arm blessing, and is the scene on the left as we face it referring to two accounts, one in the Old Testament and one in the New? Is the figure on the far left Hannah blessed by Eli and also Mary presenting her Child to us, the onlookers, while Simeon has his arm raised in blessing? Is the group of two on the right depicting Mary greeting Elizabeth? Or is the panel of four figures linking the forerunners of Jesus and his life on earth as prophet, priest and king? Or are the figures on left the High Priest with arm upraised condemning

Jesus, and on the right Pilate washing his hands while Jesus stands before him? Or could the four figures refer to the Evangelists? The next panel up is easier to interpret. Human life is costly but also ultimately joyful, as depicted here with a figure playing a harp and another blowing a wind instrument. This points us to the ancestor of Jesus, David the shepherd-king from Bethlehem, who as a boy slew Goliath and later played the harp to soothe the troubled king Saul. The psalms, thought to be composed by David, were the base of the monastic round of prayer, the whole 150 recited daily by many in the religious community on Iona. A reflection on a favourite psalm may fit here, from among the huge range of human emotions the songs cover.

Above is a scene of sacrifice, for Abraham stands at an altar, ready to kill the smaller figure, his son Isaac, believing it to be God's will. God stays Abraham's hand and has provided an alternative – the ram caught in the thicket, here carved sideways behind Isaac. The image also refers us to Jesus, another innocent son who goes, unresisting like Isaac, to his death, though unlike Isaac he is not spared. He is the Lamb that was slain, the only son of the loving Creator who allows Jesus to go through the suffering that is the cost of his full humanity, and at the hands of other humans. A pilgrim journey is a time away from the normal thicket that life has wound round us, but also assumes a return.

Above the icon of sacrifice is a large human figure accompanied by two creatures that appear to be nibbling his ears. Here we may look again for deliberate combinations of more than one biblical scene. The scene reminds us of the prophet Daniel, to whom Jesus is sometimes compared, in the lions' den (Daniel 6:10–24); while this can also be taken as Christ in the desert, among the wild beasts (Mark 1:13). Here he was tempted, as are all humans, and resisted.

Jesus is thus presented on the shaft, as prefigured in Old Testament tales, as prophet, sacrifice and king.

This leads us to the central image of the cross, presented at the meeting place of arms and shaft, within a circle. Here, surrounded by four angels, Mary presents Jesus to all onlookers. This occurred first at the Epiphany, the showing to the wise men who came from beyond ancient Israel, as told in Matthew 2:11. This represents the salvation offered to all nations told of in the Song of Simeon in Luke 2:30–32; and the Good News to be preached to the ends of the earth, in the Great Commission after the Resurrection in Matthew 28:19.

This scene is also found on a related cross at Kildonan on Islay, and closer to home on the shaft of the Saint Odhràin's Cross. As with the icons of the Orthodox tradition, there are several possible poses, each with its own focus for meditation. It can be that Mary looks at Jesus who looks outwards, blessing the nations; or Jesus looks at Mary, who in turn may look outwards to indicate Jesus to the onlooker, or she may look towards him. In each, Jesus is the core figure, larger than a human baby, the Lord of the universe as well as a nursing child. There is a hint too of the *pietà* image, in which Mary is shown as holding the body of Jesus taken down from the cross, as sketched on the coffin of the Northumbrian Saint Cuthbert. The Jesus of the Saint Odhràin's Cross turns towards Mary, head close to hers, one arm across her breast, his feet dangling like a small child's, while she appears to look outwards towards us. This image appears on the shaft of the cross, accompanied by two angels. On the Saint Martin's Cross it is not clear, after centuries of weathering, which pose is used, though Mary appears to look outwards to us, the onlookers, but her head nestles against that of Jesus and he holds her with one arm across her breast. Mother and Child accompanied by four angels occupy the central place, the crossing of the arms with the shaft, and are set in a carved ring like the mandala of an eastern icon.

At about the same time as this cross was carved the Book of Kells was made, probably on Iona too. This contains an image of Mary with Jesus (fol. 7v) surrounded by four angels; with two delightful details found on the Saint Odhràin Cross, the infant's dangly feet, and Jesus' arm across Mary's breast. The Mary of the Book of Kells looks outwards while Jesus looks at her. She is a nursing mother, her breasts clear through the image; and the angels are joyful figures, the two lower ones peering round her chair. Perhaps similar detail was once present on this cross, in the now-worn carving, or in colour painted on afterwards.

Outside the circle on the short arms and upper shaft are lions, reminiscent of the Lion of Judah, one of the images for Christ.

We are learning more about the cross and the way it relates to sunlight. There were no buildings, but many burials, nearby in early Christian and medieval times, which allowed the effects of light and shadow to be displayed on clear days, and integrated into the community's inner sense of timing on cloudy days. We know that the shadow of the replica of Saint John's Cross falls on the door of the nearby Saint Columba's Chapel, most dramatically at midsummer. At around the Feast of Martinmas, 11 November, the lengthened shadow of the Saint Martin's Cross falls on the door of Saint Columba's Chapel at about the hour of Vespers, evening prayer, which in winter is about 40 minutes before sunset, that is, about twenty minutes to four. Vespers has from ancient times included the saying of the Magnificat, the

Song of Mary, so the last image on the west face, that of Mary, has a counterpart in the words of the service. In the mornings of those short days, at about 9am, the time when physical work would start, the shadow at this time of year draws a long line down that part of the Street of the Dead, which leads to what is now the peace garden.

Like Saint Peter's shadow in the Acts of the Apostles, which brought healing to those it touched, and like the cloak of Saint Columba, the places where the shadow fell was blessed, under the protection of the saint. The Old Irish word '*scath*', 'shadow', can also mean 'shield'. So Martinmas, the feast day of the solider turned monk, in its modern form of Remembrance Day, can perhaps be considered through the layers of meaning that the Saint Martin's Cross and its shadow offer.

We may also reflect on its other uses. It was a symbol of Christ's sharing suffering with us, of hope and resurrection, near to the central holy site, the Shrine of Saint Columba. Perhaps it served as a marker too for boats crossing the Sound, to help people take note of the tides and the safest points for crossing, something that brings to mind the danger of travel on the sea today. Today it is the gathering point for the island pilgrimage, and a focus for communal and private prayer at other times. Once it had another use: visitors in 1698 and 1760 note that the islanders buried their unbaptised babies around the foot, a fitting place under the protection of Mary and her Child.

Another way of marking monastic time was the bell, a small saint's bell carried by hand, or towards the end of the Columban period, a large one rung from 'bell-towers', the round towers of Ireland and beyond. Small bells of this kind may have been among the metalwork produced on Iona. A bell called a blessing on the place where the ringing was heard. Like all religious symbolism, it was revered only there where the context was understood. In excavations at Repton in Derbyshire, where the great Viking Army of 873-874 resided, a small bell of Irish type was found, with its tongue lying close by.

An Irish bell in Derby

Emerging crushed
from the rusted earth,
could an empty bell with
a sundered tongue
recall a story
lost of its chime?

Who once poured
your molten soul,
and moulded you,
cooled, refined, rounded you,
then found your tone?

Did you then tell the way
for a wandering saint
through the long woods of Ireland,
crossing hills and strands,
blessing the land,
sounding through swaying waves
on shores and forelands,
the note of grace
in his footsteps?

Were you venerated
named and saved,
vibrating your call
among successors,
the strength of small note
singing the years?

Were you sent
across the tides
of time and nation
to bell the hours
in another land,
of other tongues?

Or were you ripped, plundered,
the ring of enslavement
wrenched to discordance,
axed in hands
unawed by your story,
greedy for toys?

Were you discarded?
Or hidden from those
who beat iron into swords?

When you rose from the wreck
of the warrior years,
your freedom wrapped
in a shroud of story;
did you yearn for the sounds
of another age?

Rosemary Power

REILIG ODHRÀIN (ORAN)

Saint Martin's Cross stands beside the sunken road made of rounded stones known as the Street of the Dead. This was part of the ancient route from Martyrs' Bay to the central part of the abbey, its stones worn and polished by countless human feet. A now-vanished gateway led through what is now a wall and directly before the gate of the chapel in the cemetery.

For many people the chapel of Reilig Odhràin (Oran) is a place where they sense deep peace. Open at all times, its plain and rather battered appearance attracts the casual view of some, while others may make it *their* place, somewhere to *be* rather than do, even in winter.

It is used for silent prayer, and sometimes it carries the sound of music, whether vocal or played on an instrument like the wooden recorder. At night many passers-by welcome the sight of the red flame flickering on the Communion table, seen through the grill of the door; or the light from candles left to burn out after a service.

In the daytime, light falls on the Communion table from two windows in the long walls – there is no east window so there was once in all likelihood a wall-painting here, which our imaginations might supply. In the corner is a cross where people pin notes that are added to the service of prayers for healing in the abbey that takes place on Tuesday evenings. In the evening we bring our own light, as our ancestors did, or sit with the dark. This is a place where the mystery of still presence before God leads to active service in the world.

It is a mortuary chapel, for the repose of the dead, and lies on the very edge of the main enclosure of the old monastic site. The protective wall of the vallum (the ditch-and-dyke marker of the central monastic site) can be seen as it passes down the hill across the road, and followed the current cemetery down to where the modern extension of the cemetery was made. The Saint Odhràin Cross may have stood at an entrance on the 'Street of the Dead', and provided a place for pilgrims to stop, reflect on the carvings and pray as they entered or left the sacred centre of the island.

The oldest building on the monastic site, earlier than the Benedictine monastery, the Reilig Odhràin Chapel reminds us how close the community on Iona was to Ireland and Irish ways, in lifestyle, liturgy and architecture. The chapel is like the early stone churches of Ireland, with a high-pitched roof, small oblong shape and a door in the west wall. At some stage in the twelfth century, the doorway was rebuilt to form the arch we see today.

Like the abbey and nunnery churches, the chapel does not face due east but some degrees to the south: it seems likely that all three were orientated towards sunrise on a particular saint's feast day. In winter this means that some extra sunlight reaches in through the south window, and on bright days sends a shaft across the floor towards the Communion table. Sensitivity to light at different times of the day and of the year was part of our ancestors' understanding of what they saw and how they saw it. The start of Genesis, where light leads on to creation and creativity, might be a passage for reflection here.

The Communion table in the Reilig Odhràin is a replacement for the original, which was moved or chipped away after the Reformation: only a tiny corner at floor level remains. By the nineteenth century the chapel was roofless, and the broken pieces of the Saint Odhràin's Cross were found here. They may have been placed here for protection when the chapel was already roofless, the image of Virgin and Child turned downwards to conceal or preserve it, for carvings on the other side have been smoothed away by water.

When the Iona Community re-roofed the chapel in 1957 there were drawings and photographs that showed enough to pitch the roof at the original level. One of the most powerful experiences people have here is the sound of music or the human voice, with vibrations that seem to curve round the walls, then linger, enveloping the listener.

As a place of prayer it is very old indeed. It is likely that there were earlier churches on this site, in a cemetery older still, which perhaps goes back to the time of Saint Columba, and is perhaps older still. Odhràin, possibly the same Saint Odhràin who is revered in the Waterford area and elsewhere in Ireland, is named as one of Columba's original twelve companions, and was the first of them to die, giving his name to the cemetery.

By the seventh century there was a major building on the abbey side of the current wall, perhaps a scriptorium where books were made and copied, while metal- and leather-working all took place nearby. The pilgrim road, the Street of the Dead, passes directly before the chapel's door before continuing south, and many feet have passed this way, of pilgrims, monks, tourists and craftspeople. The rounded stones, created when the mountains were folded in geological time, were then washed and formed by the sea, then, laid and re-laid, were polished by bare feet on their journeys, and now provide us a place where we can join with them in an inner pilgrimage.

The cemetery may have once been for the burial of members of the monastic community, but it became a secular burial ground. The chapel we see now was constructed for the local Hebridean kings and became associated with the family of Somerled of Argyll, which rose to power in the middle of the twelfth century. Some of their bones may lie under the stones, while the tombstones of their descendants, which once lay outside, are arranged along the north wall. The double-carved cross, the model for the silver Communion table cross of the abbey, is carved on one of them, another has the Tree of Life, while others have the secular symbols of their rule: the sword and the Highland galley. Whatever their lifestyle, they wanted at the end to be buried in the place made holy by the saints.

This is a place to think of death without fear. In the south wall is a late medieval tomb recess. At the apex of the stone canopy is a figure of Christ on the cross, Christ Triumphant as on the MacLean Cross, fully clothed and with arms open to embrace. Below is the symbol of the church, a head wearing an abbot's mitre, and below, now very faint, is a Green Man, a face that sprouts foliage from the mouth. He may be seen as 'speaking' the living foliage that comes from his lips, telling of renewal and regrowth, spring and resurrection. He may perhaps also be seen as singing the psalms, especially those joyful ones that celebrate the natural world. The deceased lay under the cross of the Christ of the Resurrection; the prayer of the Church; and the hope of renewal, through life beyond death. The now-vanished tomb might have served for the dawn Communion at Easter.

There are known Scots and Irish royals who were buried on Iona, and this cemetery may hold them. One of the Norse sagas tells of a reluctantly Christian poet, Hallfreðr, who died at sea and whose coffin washed to Iona, where he was buried, though it does not say where. In more recent times those buried here include the drowned crew of a nineteenth-century ship that foundered off the west side of the island; the ashes of the folk-singer and collector Marjory Kennedy-Fraser (1857–1930); a nameless seaman of the Second World War, buried near the gate closest to the abbey entrance; and the Master Mason who worked with the rebuilding of the abbey, Bill Amos (1888–1949). Islanders are still buried here, as they have been down the years, while the grave of the politician John Smith (1938–1994) is decorated by visitors with flowers, shells and stones.

The chapel and cemetery have been loved down the centuries. An early thirteenth-century poem speaks of the delight the poet had felt when he had prayed walking around the Reilig Odhràin cemetery sunwise at dawn, in the days before the Benedictine abbey was built. In the nineteenth century, when the chapel was roofless, the Free Church met in all weathers in the cemetery, before their own chapel was built at Martyrs' Bay.

For many, the chapel is very plain, and comes into its fullness through its extraordinary atmosphere conducive to prayer, whether the only sound is that of the waves on the shore and the wind; or whether the space is filled with human energy and music. In summer swallows raise their young in the rafters. The natural world is not far away in this plain, unheated chapel, with only natural light or the light people bring with them. Perhaps here too there is a sense that in praying we join with those who have prayed here before us, and have added their love, grief, joy, hope, anger and holiness to this place.

Reilig Odhràin Chapel

This place lies thick with God and centuries
of grief and rage, and plague of kin on kin,
of drownings, famine, emigration, age;
and battles fought by sword, or prayer, and pride,
by monks and warriors, weary hermits, saints
and fishermen, and women working hay.

We come, not to draw back the hardened dead,
whose story's gone beyond their battles' end,
but linger here – behind the warring years
yet touching them, here lies the quiet of Christ.

Here too one night, the air
heavy with the old,
and the waves constant on the shore behind;
here waiting for the silent word
in this place here of peace beneath the fear

there came an instant when the years dissolved
and through the open door a gust of wind
brought back a time long past
when the land lay in innocence,
blessed before chapel, hermitage or circling grove,
under grey dew, stones and stars,
with the moon glinting upon ancient daisies.

Rosemary Power

IONA NUNNERY

Further down the Street of the Dead – which passes under the gardens of the St Columba Hotel, past where the later MacLean's Cross now stands, and along the now-tarmacked road – lies one of the most loved places on Iona. The ruins of the nunnery, with its graceful, rounded architecture and modern garden, offer somewhere to sit on a warm day. The pink of the Mull granite contrasts with grey stones in the walls, and both with the slightly green limestone of the carved arches, windows and 'string course' (the decorative line that goes around the upper wall, outside and inside). The building shows evidence of fine workmanship – a lot of care was taken with establishing this church with its cloister and domestic buildings. Raised perhaps in the late twelfth century, some years before the men's Benedictine buildings, several of the church's features appear to have been copied and embellished in the abbey. The carvings on the pillars and arches are worn by wind and rain, but still visible in places; while the large windows must have always made this church a place of light which played on paintings on the now bare but once-plastered walls. The orientation some degrees south of east, meant that the maximum light possible would enter the church.

The site of Saint Ronan's Chapel, just to the north, is very old. There were once stone crosses nearby, and a pilgrim way from Martyrs' Bay to the abbey passed by its west end. The thirteenth-century ruined building we see now was once the islanders' parish church. Below it a smaller, older chapel was excavated, and below that were found older burials.

The nunnery buildings themselves went through change over time. The church was adapted in the chilly fifteenth century, when the arches to the side-aisle were blocked and a gallery put in at the west end, cutting across the main west window, both changes making the church warmer but darker. After the Reformation the nuns were allowed to live out their lives here, but then the buildings fell into decay. By the eighteenth century cows were kept in the church, and soon after 1831 the remaining roof fell in. Shortly afterwards the west wing of the cloister buildings was demolished to make way for the new island road. The ruins were stabilised in 1870, and the cloister was made into a garden in 1922.

Who were the nuns and how did they live? The first prioress, Bethóc, was a daughter of the powerful Hebridean leader Somerled. Probably born in the 1140s or 1150s, she may have been a middle-aged widow when this became her home. As the daughter of a wealthy family she would have learnt in childhood how to run a large household, but we do not know how or when she became a nun; or whether she trained in one of the Irish houses of Augustinian nuns attached to male monasteries founded in honour of Saint Columba. At a time of artistic and religious renewal and experimentation throughout Europe, Bethóc may have seen herself as reviving an older tradition of women's monastic life on the island. Recent research indicates that there may have been an earlier nunnery near Martyrs' Bay. Whether or not there were nuns here before Bethóc and her community, the site was certainly attractive to people from the earliest times. Not long ago excavations beside the school showed what appeared to be the home of farmers thousands of years earlier under the shelter of the hill.

Bethóc was certainly able to read and write, necessary skills for running a monastic community. She was the likely owner of the Iona Psalter (National Library of Scotland ms. 10000), a richly decorated copy of the psalms made in southern England in about 1200 for an Augustinian nun with an interest in Iona saints. She is also credited with founding a church on North Uist, Teampull na Trionaid, the Church of the Trinity. Some choir nuns may have come to Iona from similar backgrounds to her, while the lay-sisters, who did the more physical work of the community, may have been islanders who chose this way of life from the start, or after having raised a family and been widowed.

The names of most of the nuns, even prioresses, are not known. The community owned land in the southern part of Iona and may have kept their cows in summer by Loch Staonaig, as later islanders did. They had lands elsewhere too, including on the now-abandoned Heiskeir (Monach Islands) to the west of

Uist. They would have always been poorer than the monks and less independent, and although they probably cared for women pilgrims these were in likelihood fewer and less wealthy than their male counterparts. They may have taken in young girls of noble family for their education. Their work was considered less valuable, and most of their records have been lost.

Their way of life was a choice that freed them from the dangers of childbirth and the duties of raising a family, and would in some cases allow them to develop their innate spiritual or artistic talents. The nuns' main concern was prayer, seven times a day in the church, including in the middle of the night. Their work was to praise God and to pray for the world, for good harvests, for healing for the sick and for all those in trouble. Reciting the psalms and private prayer; reading and perhaps copying and decorating copies of Gospels; listening to the religious and other stories of their time which linked them to the wider world as they ate together; working linen and embroideries for churches; providing hospitality for pilgrims and food for the poor; listening to their stories, from distant places or close at hand; growing medicinal herbs and treating those who came to them; all these would have formed the pattern of their days. The lay sisters would have made butter and cheese, spun and woven clothing for the community, harvested the crops and foraged the shoreline for food and sources for dyes. Down the years they kept to this rhythm, until some twenty years after the Reformation the last prioress, Christina Maclean, 'with the consent of the community', perhaps by then down to two or three old ladies, gave the nunnery to the MacLeans of Duart. Perhaps that was the last piece of business transacted in the chapterhouse, where the seats still provide a place of rest and reflection for the traveller. The burial ground continued in use, but was now used for island women and their young children.

There was a way of life espoused here by the community, centred on prayer, communing with God, as the focus of existence. All daily concerns revolved around it and daily activities were its natural outcome.

One of the nuns' roles was the provision of hospitality, making a place of peace, a safe space, for those who could pay and those who could not. A place where all may contribute through their story, shared or silent, may be part of the ways in which the Christian faith is expressed in the future.

This may be a place to reflect on the often-silenced stories of women, whose names may be unknown but who have stayed faithful to the inner vision against all restrictions.

The original architecture of the nunnery is beautiful and all of a piece, finely carved and carefully planned. Some features, like the window in the side chapel, the side-chapel arch, the carvings at the heads of some pillars, were copied or amplified in the constantly redeveloped abbey. The decorative string-course that runs right around the monastic church curves upwards over the tall, rounded windows, those still standing and those that once drew light from outside; and around the frame of the east window which once held two narrow pointed windows. There are mysterious elements, like the high, narrow doorways from the cloister to the church and from the side chapel to the altar area, and the faint carving of a crozier on the pillar of the side chapel. There are traces of plaster in this side chapel, which would once have been covered with images in bright colours. The stones which once held up the fifteenth-century gallery at the west end of the chapel are carved with scenes of the Incarnation and death of Jesus.

The poem in stone which was their home remains a beloved place. Is a sense of place part of our own journeys through life, and how does it speak to us of the divine?

The cloister was extended in the fifteenth century. On the outside wall, above where the road now runs, is a sheela-na-gig, a figure designed to frighten away evil. In the field beyond, the nunnery gardens and orchards once lay, on the sunny side of the buildings. Somewhere nearby there must have been a well. To the east, the cemetery looks over the Sound of Iona and the island landing place.

Church life changes and sometimes dies. At the time it is painful, and often feels at the mercy of outside forces. It may seem that what we hold dear depends on a handful of elderly people. The nuns went through this, at the same time as the monks in the abbey, but had even less power to shape events. But their prayer has left behind in the nunnery a legacy of blessing in its harmony of peace, healing and inspiration for our own times and its needs.

Girls known to Jesus (Iona nunnery)

Jephthah's daughter
war-leader's daughter
Jairus' daughter
faith-leader's daughter
Herodias' daughter
politics' daughter –

girls with no name on the brink
of womanhood, feared
by the pure men –

and poor little poor girls
named by no one

polluted by night-work
that's no game for children –
    (Come to me, weary)
girls over the brink
of feared womanhood.

And the sick little girl
of the Gentile woman
and Naaman's small slave-girl
lost to her parents –

girls read and met
on the Way to the Hill;

and all the chances
lost to creation
in broken young girls
on the wheels of a world
driven by pure men,
permitted by most folk;

and a girl named Mary
on the brink of her marriage
making the choices
of risks in the changing
of base coin to gold.

Here Jesus knew daughters
of good folk and rough folk,
the milkers of cattle,
the ladies in choir,
the makers of coarse cloth,

the weavers of fine work,
the cloth for the altar
determined by pure men;

girls entering cloister
under the arches
containing their new world
of feared womanhood;

their risking, their choosing
their reading, their hearing
of meetings with girls
on the Way to the Hill;

with gossiping, gaming,
sickening and praying,
their seeking the freedom
to meet in the soul,

now nameless, forgotten,
their spindles decaying,
their weaving has rotted,

with only a prioress
or two on a tombstone,

and bones known to God.

In this quiet place we hear,
under gracious arches
and open skies,
echoes of silenced steps

of stable lives, lost stories
where daughters to priests
and politicians, war-leaders,
raiders, followers, poor folk,
the old wanting rest on
the Way to the Hill,
running or reluctant, found their home,
gave hospitality, sacrifice to God

where energy transmuted into peace,
has left unspeaking holiness in stone.

Rosemary Power

THE COW IN THE CROSSING

Returning to the abbey, we can sit in the Benedictine church, allowing all that is happening around us to take its course. One of the joys about pilgrimage is in finding that stories which have given us pleasure have also inspired others over centuries. The feast day of Saint Adomnán of Iona, the seventh-century abbot, is 23 September.

Adomnán wrote a book about the holy places of Jerusalem based on information from a pilgrim visiting Iona. On the basis of this work Iona is thought, though it stood at the far ends of the earth, to have been viewed as a more local model for the centre of Christian worship, Jerusalem, the place of the suffering, Resurrection and the Second Coming of Christ. Iona as a place of pilgrimage was already established for over a hundred years when Adomnán wrote *On the Holy Places*: now he increased its significance for those who could not spend years on the road to Jerusalem, but could visit the northern European New Jerusalem closer to home.

Adomnán's best-known book today is his *Life of Saint Columba*. In this, Adomnán tells many stories of his predecessor which underpin his later legal writing. One concerns a young slave-girl who is savagely killed when clinging to the student Columba for protection, and the anger the young saint felt at the violation of her humanity. He tells of how, on Iona, Columba himself ground grain to provide food for visitors, taking on himself the humblest, hardest work, which was elsewhere the role of slave-women.

In 697 Adomnán produced another work, *The Law of the Innocents*, which was accepted by the main secular and religious leaders of Ireland and western Scotland. It protected non-combatants in warfare and exempted from military service women, clerics and children. Adomnán was building on Gaelic tradition: an earlier law ascribed to Saint Patrick forbade the killing of clerics, while the law of the nun Dáire forbade the killing of cattle, which were the basic unit of wealth, and which were the source of food, especially for the young and the weak. Prayer combined with practical action for justice in the case of these three lawmakers.

A starting-place for meditation may be on these laws, the slow struggle towards justice for the oppressed, and the needs of just law today, for those in modern slavery in our own economy, for those who are in most need.

Another story in the *Life of Saint Columba* tells of how Columba, in Ireland, had owned a cow, from which he provided his cats with milk, until it was stolen. The image on the capital (head) of the central south-east chancel pillars faces into the nave of Iona Abbey, the place where laypeople and pilgrims stood during services. Perhaps once brightly painted, it now benefits from the lighting of our own time. We see a cow, which, in defiance of Dáire's law, is being forcibly taken and doomed for slaughter. These carvings reflect on contemporary practice, for when they were made in the fifteenth century cattle-rustling in the Highlands and Islands was commonplace. Here is a story, in full view of the rich and poor who came to pray in the nave. A man on his knees, just visible on the far left of the photograph (p.46), dressed in the traditional garb of the poor, raises his hands to heaven. Another man, in the stylish dress of the fifteenth century, a short tunic and long hood, drives off the poor man's cow, holding it by the tail. Another man, also fashionably-clad, holds the cow's head, while a third stands ready with an axe. The fate of the cow, and the man whose family depends on it, is on view at this dramatic moment.

God heard the prayers of Saint Columba for his cow in Adomnán's story, and now God, who sees all acts, hears the prayers of Columba. The pilgrims stand under Columba's protection, and he demands that the poor be treated justly. For a pilgrim in the nave this image says that if you are one of the poor, who has been subject to the theft of a beloved and necessary domestic animal, pray to Columba for aid, for he has known your trouble, and he will ask God to protect you and allow justice to be done. Indeed, the poor man on the left could be interpreted as Columba himself, asking God for help.

In Adomnán's story, the cow was restored unharmed to the saint. In all events God will demand redress from malefactors: the wealthy who stand side by side with the poor as pilgrims hearing the Word of God see this carving and are being called to account. They are seeking Columba's protection as pilgrims now, and trust Columba to aid them at the hour of death, but in the meanwhile they must return to life in the world, and they are required to act there justly if they are to benefit from the protection they seek. The stories of the saint, like the Gospels themselves, are intended for all listeners, to bring people back to doing right. In our century, as climate changes and people flee wars or suffer under unjust international trade rules, the challenge to our complicity is the same as it was for fifteenth-century cattle-thieves or seventh-century listeners to the *Life of Saint Columba*.

As in the scriptures, Adomnán's story was intended as a guide to conduct in the hearer's own time. This one echoes the story of the cow in the *Life of Columba*, but it also gives a local context to the tale the prophet Nathan told King David in 2 Samuel 12:1–14, about the abuse of power, in this case by the king himself. There was a man who owned a single lamb, which was a pet for his children, but a wealthy neighbour with many sheep killed the poor man's lamb to feed his own guests. By knowing the scriptural stories, and seeing them told through images, we connect to the cries for justice in our own time and place.

Above the cow is another image that takes the theme of freedom from oppression further, for a hunting dog chases a leaping hare. The hare is used in places like the Book of Kells as an image of Christ. Here, the beauty and strength of Christ wins out against violence, and, as Psalm 91 (verses 3–4) tells us, we too can with God escape from the snare of the hunter who wishes to destroy us, or the plague that lays waste at noon.

Nearby carvings show that the God of the land animals, wild or domesticated, is also God of the birds of the air, two of which have their necks entwined. Near them too, among strange mythic creatures that are no longer understood, is the perfect image of a seahorse (at the far right of the photograph), on the same scale as the cow. The birds of the air, the creatures of the land and the dwellers of the sea are all part of God's creation. So are the human figures who act for good or ill.

Adomnán wrote the *Life of Saint Columba* knowing that in his time, there was the need for justice for the poor. It was as relevant to the medieval pilgrim as to the people of later ages, when cows are no longer the units of currency, and for most of us no longer the source of essential food. Perhaps the image and the story behind it become the more poignant in a world of climate change and polluted oceans, where multinationals strip the natural world of its resources to worship a god of profit in place of the God of love.

The following was written about a carved quernstone with an elaborate cross found at another island monastic site, which, like Iona, also suffered much from the raids of Vikings. Such a stone was probably used for hand-grinding the best grain for Communion bread.

Holy island quernstone

Carved with cross, from Inis Cultra in Lough Derg, Co. Clare, this is now in the Clare Museum, Ennis.

When slow tools worked
to cross the quern
did you sense the turn
of centuries of summer
ground where brown grain fell,
dried, refined, whitened
for heaven's gain

like bones of souls
who wrote, prayed, paid
the ordered price
of life apart
in sanctuary
then rested here to wait
another wakening?

And did you carve the lines that flow through years
and smooth the empty place to pour
the gift for all who came –
between two weights, once work of women bent
like sheaves with labour, then
recalling pain of strangers –
and times when all things stored
were torched and taken, broken, stolen

all but bones ground fine to make
the bread with bitter herbs the way
through deserts where
the grinding journey breaks

in each age, here,
and elsewhere?

Rosemary Power

FOR UNDERSTANDING AMONG THE NATIONS

A sculpture, *The Descent of the Spirit*, was placed in 1959 at the centre of the rebuilt medieval cloisters, and has served as a focus for visitors, an inspiration for reflection, and a climbing frame for children ever since.

This is not a carving, but a robust moulded bronze work, a product of the years that followed the Second World War. The Lithuanian artist Jacob Lipchitz (1891-1973) was working in Paris at the time of the Nazi Occupation. He fled and reached the United States.

The inscription integrated into the sculpture reads:

Jacob
Lipchitz
Juif fidèle
à la foi de ses ancêtres
a fait cette Vierge pour
la bonne entente des
hommes sur la terre afin
Que l'Esprit règne

Jacob Lipchitz, a Jew true to the faith of his ancestors, has made this Virgin for good understanding [la bonne entente] among the peoples of the earth. That the Spirit reign.

At the apex of the sculpture is a dove, descending, with eyes open, aware of the joy and the cost, its beak holding what the Spirit breathes into being: the star-studded canopy of the universe. This is open, displaying the main figure, who is as yet blind, but with arms open in welcome and with a deep groove between the top of her head and her womb. This is the Mary of the Incarnation, also reminiscent of the Adam of Michelangelo's

Sistine Chapel ceiling, awaiting God's call to life.

The Virgin is the representative of humanity and the focus of creation, sheltered by it, the one from whom, as she receives the Spirit, is to flow the fullness of creation. She is the product of God's primeval Word: 'Let there be light'; the creative emanation of God that is ancient Wisdom; Eve called at the start of time to steward with Adam all creation; and Mary of Nazareth. With her starry mantle she is also the woman giving birth in Revelation; and in all ages the creativity of humanity that mirrors the creativity of the God who creates.

Holding her up are four other figures, stretching upwards, part of the whole creation yearning and groaning in one great act of giving birth, as the Letter to the Romans (8:22–23) describes it. Three creatures are winged but with human-like bodies, sightless and with the same groove, open to the Spirit. The other is a lamb, token of the flock of Abel and of the Good Shepherd, open-eyed, the Lamb who was slain. The lower parts of the winged creatures fuse with the elongated body of the lamb, which is coiled, serpent-like. They reach up together from the common primeval swamp from which we have emerged and evolved, into which God the Creator entered, the Creator entering creation. Perhaps the serpent of temptation whom the Virgin of Revelation crushes is implicit in creation from the beginning. Only the open-eyed one of the four figures, the lamb, is aware from the beginning of the cost of entering into a creation that carries primeval sin. Perhaps the artist suggests that the whole – the blind and seeing, the striving and holding back, the serpent and the lamb – are within us all, and from which we are called, as we grow upwards in our personal evolution. We are people of the earth, coming from the same root, drawn at our best to receiving the Spirit from above, wildly embracing its power, for the goodness of the nations. There is a unity, a growing upwards, a life-giving optimism, portrayed by an artist who escaped the violence of the Nazi regime and the deportation of Jews from Paris to the death camps.

The underlying unity of creation is depicted in its origins and in its aspirations. The sculpture harmonises with the medieval remains and the carvings on the rebuilt cloister arches. When children play on the sculpture the harmony of creation is heard in laughter. Playfully, the bird with the bag in its beak is like the stork who delivers the new baby.

Border presentation

The following reflects on the Border between the two parts of Ireland created in the early twentieth century and the scene of killings during the thirty-year Troubles of the later twentieth century. The image of flaming towers of prayer comes from medieval Irish texts, and is based, we may assume, on the Irish round towers.

Did they walk that fortieth day –
      the baby heavier by the mile –
from Monaghan to Armagh
to present a child
destined for fall and rise
of many on the crossing?

Did she breastfeed by checkpoints,
lulling him to smile
and sleep as they metered
the lengthening road?
Did they recall in lament

roadside corpses, hope's carrion,
hear the widow and orphan
by the burnt post?

Was it further and harder,
the checkpoint simpler
than crossing the concrete
between Bethlehem and temple?

When they walked the steep streets,
through three holy circles,
was the child blessed
by the damaged hands
of mercy's prophets who
saw hope as the hounds
licked the city's wounds?

Did the system delay them,
foot-weary and wary,
waiting lifts in the twilight,
from strangers and neighbours?

Did they find with that baby
in hope that long Friday
no dreary steeples
but towers, broken but flaming,
beckoning charity,
peace opening the door?[1]

Rosemary Power

THE WORD THROUGH OTHERS

Iona prayers from recent times

DEEP PEACE OF THE RUNNING WAVE

Deep peace of the running wave to you.
Deep peace of the flowing air to you.
Deep peace of the quiet earth to you.
Deep peace of the shining stars to you.
Deep peace of the Son of Peace to you.

This well-known prayer has long been associated with Iona and has also gone far beyond, to be used throughout the English-speaking world. It appears in places as diverse as the Iona Abbey Worship Books, the Baptist funeral liturgy and, with changes to the last line, the works of the modern Pagan movement. John Rutter adapted it and set it to music. Frequently described as an ancient Celtic prayer, it takes its inspiration from the Celtic Twilight Movement of the late nineteenth century, and especially the folk traditions of the *Carmina Gadelica*, the Hebridean folk prayers collected and translated by Alexander Carmichael (1832–1912).

Exploring the prayer's history cannot destroy what it means to people, but can deepen the understanding of the words, and of our own creative impulses. We may wish to read it aloud and savour the poetry first simply for what the prayer says to us as heard.

For those who wish, a second activity can involve looking at the origins of a poem to enter a study in the ways of the creative gift of the imagination.

The lines derive from a longer poem composed on Iona in about 1900 by the writer William Sharp (1855–1905) who, towards the end of his life, spent extensive periods on the island at a time when many Celtic Revival artists were also resident during the summers. Sharp produced work as Fiona Macleod, and under this name became a prominent figure of the Celtic Revival. He had learnt Gaelic, and was, like the Irish poet W.B. Yeats, a member of the esoteric Order of the Golden Dawn. He moved during his lifetime from a spirituality based on classical nature paganism to a position much more sympathetic to the Christian Gospel but viewed from a feminine perspective, and he even suggested, ahead of his time, that Christ at the Second Coming would be in female form. His repertoire of plays, poems and reflective material from his island years was published by his widow Elizabeth in 1907, and was republished several times in the following years.

In 1947 Marian McNeill published part of a long narrative sequence by Sharp, which he attributed to a Gaelic original by Alan *dall*, with the implication that Sharp was merely the translator.

The relevant lines of the longer poem read:

Deep peace of the running wave to you;
Deep peace of the flowing air to you;
Deep peace of the quiet earth to you;
Deep peace of the sleeping stones to you;
Deep peace of the Yellow Shepherd to you;
Deep peace of the Wandering Shepherdess to you;
Deep peace from the Flock of Stars to you!

Deep peace from the Son of Peace,
Deep peace from the heart of Mary to you,
    And from Bridget of the Mantle

> Deep peace, deep peace!
> And with the kindness, too, of the Haughty Father
>   Peace!
> In the name of the Three who are One,
>   Peace!
> And by the will of the King of the Elements,
>   Peace, Peace!

From Iona: An Anthology

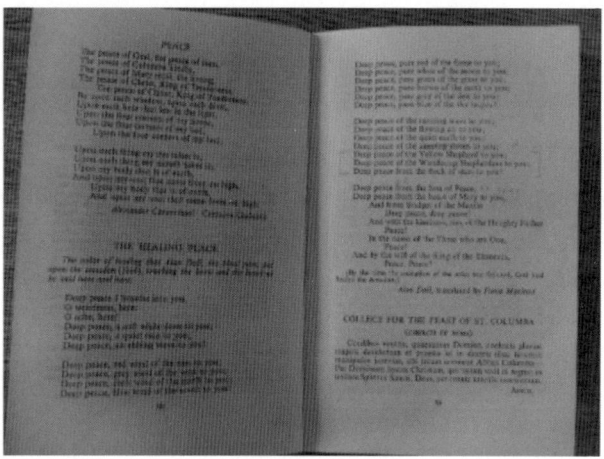

A copy of the 1952 second edition of McNeill's *Iona: An Anthology*, published by the Iona Community, is in the Iona Cathedral library in the abbey. Someone has neatly made changes in pencil to form the well-known prayer that has been extracted and adapted from the lines by Sharp as Fiona Macleod. Whether this was done by the original adapter, or whether it was done to conform to what was already in use on Iona, is not clear. The hand is not that of George MacLeod, the founder of the Iona

Community, nor of Ralph Morton, the Deputy Leader, but the way it has been done shows how, in the atmosphere of Iona liturgy and worship, someone worked with the lines to fit the mood of the time.

In the prayer we know, the sleeping stones have vanished, as have the Yellow Shepherd and the Wandering Shepherdess, while the flock of stars has become the shining stars. Sharp's closing note on this section of his much longer narrative poem shows that he saw the verses as a prayer that took the form of a religious charm, with the recitation of the *eolas* (knowledge) leading to God healing the Fool (Amadan), a figure who occurs in the wider context of the work. This narrative poem would have had little interest to those who saw, however, how a few of the lines fitted the robust but poetic Christianity espoused by George MacLeod and his followers.

Sharp, as Fiona Macleod, attributes this poem to a Gaelic original from a recognised poet. Ailean *dall*, Blind Alan, MacDougall (c.1750–1828) was well-known in Lochaber, and fifty-four of his fifty-six known works were published, either in 1798 or after his death in 1829. As the Gaelic scholar Ronald Black has shown, his subjects were primarily elegies and eulogies. There were also songs about women; six poems about ships; two about drink (one for and one against); two about snuff; and, perhaps his best-known work, a satire on Lowland shepherds. We learn from his repertoire that he liked steamboats, women, drink and tobacco but disliked Lowlanders and sheep. He was inclined to take a traditional approach to poetry in Gaelic. There is no sense that he was enamoured of the Celtic romance of James Macpherson, leader of the eighteenth-century outburst of all things Celtic. Ailean *dall* is known to have addressed religious matters only in two verses of one of his later poems, an elegy on a Cameron Colonel killed at Waterloo, and even there the main focus is a veiled criticism of the War Office.

It is hard to imagine that this poem comes from the rumbustious Ailean *dall*, and much more likely that it is Sharp's own work, and that, like Macpherson before him, he constructed an imaginary Gaelic original. It is one of his own compilations, influenced by Alexander Carmichael's translations of the *Carmina Gadelica* in both its rhythm and content.

Sharp included a Yellow Shepherd, and this may have been inspired, consciously or not, by a mountain of that name, Aonach Buidhe in Kintail. The Wandering Shepherdess may be there purely for the balance of the sexes, but if she has any literary origins they could include the glimmering girl who called and then vanished in Yeats' 1890s poem 'Song of the Wandering Aengus'. But Aengus becomes old with wandering as he seeks her, so she is hardly an agent of peace. Yeats both admired the writings of Fiona Macleod and detested William Sharp, unaware that they were the same person. Sharp's views on Yeats are unknown, but if the animosity was mutual, any use of this poem as a source may well have been unconscious.

While the Iona adaptation of some lines for liturgical prayer became more widely known, the longer original sequence from William Sharp's poem also retained a readership.

The immediately preceding five lines of the longer poem appear in the Corrymeela Community Worship Book of 1981:

Deep peace, pure green of the grass to you.
Deep peace, pure white of the moon to you.
Deep peace, pure brown of the earth to you.

Deep peace, pure grey of the dew to you.
Deep peace, pure blue of the sky to you.

These are followed by the lines adapted and known on Iona.

The process of adaptation has a communal aspect, and since the prayer found its current form it has been used in liturgies ever since. None of the exploration of its past affects the capacity of the prayer to touch many hearts. The original author, William Sharp, may have learnt in eternity with astonishment and delight how far his works had been compressed and adapted, the creative process started on Iona continuing beyond his time on earth. It seems appropriate that among its many uses the 'Deep peace' prayer is prayed and sung around the world. It also remains part of our Morning Prayer at its original home on Iona.

Prayer for writers

Our Columba, hope of Scots,
hear us as we labour.

When we are called
to take the oar in hand,
put the curragh to the waves
and be wafted by words
where we would not journey
but with God's Spirit.

Hear us, Jesus,
when youth is strong in us
and you are our courage
as we adventure on the sea.

Hear us as we seek
for learning, like the rippling
of sunlight on calm waters.
May we remember what
you wish us to record.

Fill our sails with wind
full with yearning
for the land beyond our sight.

And hear us
when we bail the boat,
spilling the bilge that drowns.
Free us from what we want:
that in work we find your desires.

Help us on the cross
of ropes that catch the words then bind us.
And when we loathe the labour you have given us
help us weather the weariness
and come through storm
to find you before us
as you add our catch to the feast.

Rosemary Power

PRAYER FOR OUR OWN RESHAPING

O God, who gave to your servant Columba
the gifts of courage, faith and cheerfulness,
and sent people forth from Iona
to carry the word of your gospel to every creature:
grant, we pray, a like spirit to your church,
even at this present time.
Further in all things the purpose of our community,
that hidden things may be revealed to us,
and new ways found to touch the hearts of all.
May we preserve with each other sincere charity and peace,
and if it be your holy will, grant that this place of your abiding
be continued still to be a sanctuary and a light.
Through Jesus Christ. Amen.

This prayer is first found, in these cadences but in the more archaic wording then deemed suitable, in the second issue of the Iona Community's magazine, *Coracle*, published in 1939. This prayer was perhaps composed by Ralph Morton, and in all events comes from the very early days of the Community, the time of rebuilding the abbey.

MacLeod had already made a name for himself for his work in deprived areas of Glasgow during the interwar years, and his plan, with Morton and his other associates, was to provide work for unemployed tradesmen with the rebuilding of the abbey. There was the wider, international context as well. The prayer was written during the Nazi period in Europe, when its horrors were already well-known, and Germany was expanding forcibly into neighbouring countries. It was a time when the churches as institutions were more or less conforming to their nation's politics, and where those who stood out against wrong were publicly vilified, arrested, and were often rejected by their churches as well. Starting to rebuild a medieval abbey at this time was a major act of faith, and the prayer presents it as far from an inward-looking one.

It professes a 'Protestant' version of sainthood: the One addressed is God, and Columba is not invoked but is regarded as a model for the Christian, someone prayerful and graced by God in the spreading of the Word. He was given, we are told, courage, faith and cheerfulness, the last an aspect of the renewal of faith that MacLeod emphasised as an essential ingredient of Christianity, but one that has often been lost to sight in church life.

God is asked to further the work of the new Community that has been set up to emulate that of the original monastery, in both its immediate and its future, then unknown, work. The founders of the Iona Community hoped that, as the monastery was rebuilt, people would be built up spiritually on Iona, an island that has continually been a focus for prayer. This prayerfulness had led, at the start of the twentieth century, to the restoration of the Abbey Church as a place for worship by members of any Christian denomination. At a time when the darkness of war was coming to all Europe, the prayer asks that Iona might remain a place which draws people, a sanctuary and a light, from which the light of the Gospel can be sent out through people touched by Iona. In times of plenty and times of hardship, this has been the case, and now, as the enormity of the climate crisis and our international inaction comes home to us, it may be a valuable prayer for many people, that we may face the future with courage, faith and cheerfulness as we care for our neighbour.

Change and renewal have been part of the island's story, and are part of the current prayer. The words but not the cadences were adapted as styles of prayer became less formal and the old 'thou' forms were abandoned, and slight changes have been made in recent years as well. Saint Columba's monastery finished its work in 1203 and the work of the succeeding Benedictine community as well as that of the nunnery ended in the mid-sixteenth century, both after centuries of service to pilgrim and resident alike. The future is in God's plan, not ours, according to the prayer, but the courage, faith and cheerfulness attributed to Saint Columba are to be part of what the people who have been built up with their rebuilding of the abbey will take with them.

The prayer has long survived the completion of the buildings, and is used when Members of the Iona Community meet together, and by Associates, Friends, staff and guests. It may be as relevant as ever now when, after the recent renovation of the residential areas, followed by the pandemic, the Iona Community is exploring new ways of ensuring that they are used in a manner that honours the original vision, in ways that touch our society today. It is one of the core prayers of the Community, central to the spirituality of a twentieth-century movement with its heart in the ancient place where its task of rebuilding took place.

Iona visitors

They come on days
so grey the sea may
heave to shores they waited
years to see
but now must hear;
or come of curiosity
to pay brief praise
where old monks stayed,
and raised the cross
of grace,
then faded into shadow
and still bless the place.

Where once they prayed
the heritage remains,
and those who stay
listen to hear,
sounding through centuries of search
and pilgrimage of time,
seasons of grace,
and know they tread again on holy ground.

Rosemary Power

THE MASTER CARPENTER

O Christ, the Master Carpenter,
who, at the last, through wood and nails,
purchased our whole salvation,
wield well your tools
in the workshop of your world,
so that we who come rough-hewn to your bench
may here be fashioned
to a truer beauty of your hand.
We ask it for your own name's sake. Amen.

One of the best-loved prayers associated with the Iona Community is this perfectly honed poem where every word counts for the cadences and the biblical imagery that express a radical Christian theology. The crux of the prayer is that we might take the step of allowing Christ to heal and shape us into what we are intended to be, an act of trust that in turns allows us to serve others.

Selected by George MacLeod in the early days of the Iona Community, and given the title 'Prayer for our own reshaping', it has itself been reshaped from earlier material. A Scout Prayer popular in the 1930s attributed to Martin P.G. Leonard (1889–1963) reads:

> *O Jesu, Master Carpenter, who at the last through wood and nails purchased our whole redemption, wield well thy tools in this thy workshop, that we who come rough-hewn may be fashioned to a nobler beauty by thy hand: for thy name's sake, O Jesus Christ our Lord. Amen.*

Leonard had a background not unlike MacLeod's own military one. He won the Distinguished Service Order as a First World

War chaplain, then worked for TocH, a Christian movement for ex-soldiers and young people; and was later Provost of St Mary's Cathedral, Glasgow. He may have written this prayer, but it is possible that it was older, and originally composed in the late nineteenth century by a public-school teacher, cleric and Fellow of Oriel College, Oxford, Arthur Gray Butler (1831–1909), a brother-in-law of the social reformer Josephine Butler.

Wherever it first came from, and how many were involved in creating this 'Prayer for our own reshaping', the reworked poetic form known across the English-speaking world took shape slowly within the Iona Community. Apart from its beauty and apparent simplicity, the prayer displays how MacLeod's own theology had moved from the Calvinism of his Church of Scotland background to an acceptance of an approach more akin to the Eastern Orthodox Church. The form has similarities to prayers from early Christian Ireland and Hebridean folk prayers.

The prayer addresses Christ through his trade. He is a Master Carpenter, one proficient in his skill to a level that allows apprentices to be taken on. The term is also used, again for both sexes, in academic life for a higher degree which traditionally conferred teaching status, a matter which would have been as clear to an academic like Gray as its manual alternative was to any skilled tradesperson. This is God incarnate among ordinary people, with gifts like theirs which can be honed. Our salvation is his last, best work, the one at the end of his earthly life, in which Jesus engages through the final act of self-giving, of placing us before himself. He completes the pattern of his creation even through the suffering which is the cost of following his work on earth.

We can take it further: we are all called to participate in the redemptive process, and the skillfulness we develop in our own forms of work engages us in its accomplishment. To MacLeod and his contemporaries this would have been particularly pointed as they attempted to cross social boundaries and work physically with the manually skilled, enabling the abbey to be rebuilt. The prayer's continuing popularity suggests that others have since found in the prayer this sense of contributing to the work of our own, and the world's, salvation, the 'whole salvation' of the next phrase.

Christ uses wood to its best effect, for its beauty and its usefulness, and the prayer comes to this image through the crucifixion, where the tools of Christ's creative trade are turned against him, distorted to destroy life.

While this prayer may be intensely comforting to some who have been wounded by life, the imagery of 'purchased our whole salvation' may at first sight repel others. The word 'purchased' can echo the severe forms of Calvinism and its distortions which view the suffering of the cross as punishment, an understanding in which Jesus is substituted for ourselves, willingly taking on the pain on our behalf for a God who demands retribution and requires a penalty, rather than a God who offers mercy and shares the pain of our lives. The harsher interpretation makes the rest of the prayer impossible, but it is only a small minority of Christians who subscribe to the concept, and the beliefs of the majority with less violent understandings of atonement give us much more richness. The Greek word δικαιοσύνη, which we often translate as 'justice', and in consequence carries legalistic overtones, can also be translated as 'righteousness'. This is the opposite of self-righteousness, and means the much more positive 'being made right' with God. This nuance of meaning is even stronger in the Hebrew, where being 'at-right' with God features repeatedly. This at-one-ment, to use the English word created by the first translators of the Bible, provides a gentler approach to the phrase 'purchased our whole salvation'.

The image thus has resonances not with punishment inflicted on the innocent but with the pearl of great price, acquired at cost by the joyful merchant. It may refer to the ancient tradition of humans being 'purchased' and freed from Satan. This developed from the images used by Saint Paul of humans being 'redeemed' or 'ransomed' in the same way that captives in war or slaves were paid for, an echo of the humiliation of Jesus, whose betrayal was paid for at thirty pieces of silver, the normal price of a slave. A slave longs for freedom, and here Jesus, in taking the place of the slave, is understood as freeing that person, who has been slave to sin. He then shows freedom in the way he undertakes his own Passion by crucifixion, a punishment inflicted upon slaves and for those deemed by the Romans to deserve it. In the Resurrection Jesus not only displays his freedom but enables everyone else to be free, including those enslaved in other ways, such as addiction to money, sex or power. This in turn takes some to the other meaning of 'purchase': to grip, take hold of, to attract like a magnet.

It is possible also to take the view of 'purchase' and atonement developed in the twelfth century by Peter Abelard, that the suffering of Jesus is not what God demands but what we humans need. The God of compassion suffers with us, goes through our own painful passions with us through the Calvary that exists throughout time and place. We can in turn join our own sufferings to the sufferings of Christ, for our own healing and for the good of the world in ways that may never be known on earth. It takes us also to the understanding that the redemptive process engaged not only the death of Jesus but his whole life on earth, in his work, companionship, teaching and actions.

Christ is in this prayer the carpenter-joiner actively engaged with the Creator, in his own and Jewish terminology, his father; and, in the ministry which eventually and inevitably led to people destroying him 'at the last'. Not a passive victim, he allowed this to happen and in doing so 'purchased our whole salvation'.

For others, the word remains a problem and has been changed to 'accomplished' or 'crafted', though in doing so the image is lost of Jesus being sold for the price of a slave, of someone who desired freedom, and is thus gaining it. For myself I use the word 'prepared', for a redemption, and a sharing of suffering that is offered but not enforced by the God of courtesy.

Joining our own suffering to that of the God of love on the cross was a theme found in the writings of early Ireland at the time of Columba and later. It returns in folk prayers, one of which, cited in part by Helen Waddell in her novel *Peter Abelard*, reads:

O King of Friday
whose limbs were stretched on the cross,
O Lord who did suffer
the wounds for the many, the loss;
we place ourselves
beneath the shade of your might –
may some fruit from the tree of your Passion
fall on us this night.[2]

'Wield well your tools in the workshop of your world' would be an impossible prayer without the ingredient of choice in love and the knowledge that Christ is skilled at what he is doing. Within that context it can be a plea for Christ's action in places where the tools of our own trades are wielded wrongly, by ourselves, or when they are in the hands of murderers, torturers, embezzlers. It becomes a prayer for justice, for the reshaping of God's world.

'That we who come rough-hewn to your bench' is at once more personal, acknowledging that, though originally conceived as works of art, precious in the sight of the Maker, we are rough-hewn, hacked about by circumstances, personal sin and the actions of other human beings. This is where the prayer appears to move to trust that the carpenter will find beauty that no amount of violence can deface. Christ the carpenter is portrayed as artist, displaying the true grain of the wood, and the uses to which it can best be shaped.

This is at the heart of the prayer: we ask for the courage to take the risk of being changed, to allow our hurts to become part of the grain and the strength of the wood. The prayer allows us to lay aside our autonomy to become active participants in allowing God to work with us in our reshaping, freed from the passive domination of our own will, letting ourselves be re-formed for the delight of the artist-craftsperson, and for wider use in the world. It is allowing ourselves to be part of the house of God, fulfilling God's work on earth, being joined in unexpected ways to the other people implied in the 'we', prepared in the 'truer beauty' as beams, lintels, doorsteps, rooftrees, parts of the body that are the temple and indwelling of Christ. The prayer is, by its nature, communal, composed like the Lord's Prayer in the plural 'we'.

To say 'may here be fashioned to a truer beauty of your hand' takes trust, a move to see God as working with us rather than on us, an active joining of our will to that of a God who causes no unnecessary suffering, undergoes the pain of reshaping with us and experiences the joy of the truer beauty that reflects our artistry as well as our purpose. In creating our own works of art there is always labour, pruning, rewriting, repainting, rethinking how to work with the medium we use, often for a result beyond our own expectation. Christ the artist works on us in the same ways.

Christ, the carpenter-joiner, followed the prompting of the Spirit into something greater, that led to a hideous death wrought by the tools he had worked with, but dying in a manner that formed something more beautiful and more durable from his life. This prayer can be seen as an invitation to join in this work, using our skills to the full, though at times our knowledge and tools may appear to be used against us, trusting in something bigger and ultimately with purpose.

This is a prayer to the Christ reshaping the world to the desire of a gentle Creator, a God who bears all the cost and invites us to be part of the work. The crux is that we ask it for Christ's own name's sake, echoing the words of John's Gospel (14:13), that anything we ask in his name he will provide.

Perhaps the attraction of the prayer, beautifully honed as a work of art with all the lucidity and depth of a work of art, is that it is primarily a prayer about the Incarnation, a radical invitation to the Christ to work in our own lives and, through us, the life of the world.

78 *The gift of stillness*

I BIND UNTO MYSELF TODAY

I bind unto myself today
The strong Name of the Trinity,
By invocation of the same,
The Three in One and One in Three.

I bind this day to me for ever,
By power of faith, Christ's incarnation;
His baptism in the Jordan River;
His death on Cross for my salvation;
His bursting from the spicèd tomb;
His riding up the heavenly way;
His coming at the day of doom;
I bind unto myself today.

I bind unto myself the power
Of the great love of the cherubim;
The sweet 'well done' in judgment hour,
The service of the seraphim,
Confessors' faith, Apostles' word,
The Patriarchs' prayers, the Prophets' scrolls,
All good deeds done unto the Lord,
And purity of virgin souls.

I bind unto myself today
The virtues of the starlit heaven,
The glorious sun's life-giving ray,
The whiteness of the moon at even,
The flashing of the lightning free,
The whirling wind's tempestuous shocks,

The stable earth, the deep salt sea,
Around the old eternal rocks.

I bind unto myself today
The power of God to hold and lead,
His eye to watch, His might to stay,
His ear to hearken to my need.
The wisdom of my God to teach,
His hand to guide, His shield to ward,
The word of God to give me speech,
His heavenly host to be my guard.

Against the demon snares of sin,
The vice that gives temptation force,
The natural lusts that war within,
The hostile men that mar my course;
Or few or many, far or nigh,
In every place and in all hours,
Against their fierce hostility,
I bind to me these holy powers.

Against all Satan's spells and wiles,
Against false words of heresy,
Against the knowledge that defiles,
Against the heart's idolatry,
Against the wizard's evil craft,
Against the death wound and the burning,
The choking wave and the poisoned shaft,
Protect me, Christ, till Thy returning.

Christ be with me, Christ within me,
Christ behind me, Christ before me,

Christ beside me, Christ to win me,
Christ to comfort and restore me.
Christ beneath me, Christ above me,
Christ in quiet, Christ in danger,
Christ in hearts of all that love me,
Christ in mouth of friend and stranger.

I bind unto myself the Name,
The strong Name of the Trinity;
By invocation of the same.
The Three in One, and One in Three,
Of Whom all nature hath creation,
Eternal Father, Spirit, Word:
Praise to the Lord of my salvation,
Salvation is of Christ the Lord.

Cecil Frances Alexander

This hymn is sung by many around Saint Patrick's Day, and in Iona Abbey when new members of the Iona Community become hallowed into full membership. It is long and complex to sing in full, involving two separate melodies and a change of key, so three of the original nine verses are rarely included.

The source is a ninth-century hymn in Old Irish, which was turned into verse in the space of a week by one of Ireland's most prolific nineteenth-century writers, Cecil Frances Alexander. It comes to us through the work of many people before it reached her, and at the age of seventy, with no knowledge of the Irish language, she versified it in English, preparing it for the composer who gave us the music.

Cecil Frances Alexander, née Humphreys (1818–1895), was

born in Dublin and was of English extraction. From a comfortable position in middle-class society, and influenced by the High-Church Anglican Oxford Movement, she spent her twenties engaging in one of the few acceptable public activities for women of her class, writing hymns and poems. These found a wide audience, and a few of her works, in spite of some clunky lines, are still sung today: many churchgoers will recognise 'Jesus calls us o'er the tumult/of our life's wild, restless sea' without knowing the source. Her popular 1848 collection, *Hymns for Little Children*, includes 'the green hill far away/without a city wall', and the carol service essential 'Once in Royal David's City'. 'All things bright and beautiful' is sung at pram-services, weddings and funerals, though without the second verse which declaims that 'the rich man in his castle/the poor man at his gate/God made them, high and lowly/and ordered their estate'. This exclusion, so necessary today, misses the social context of the time, and the challenge that the writer laid down. Few of us believe that God has ordered our society in this manner, but she is referring to the parable of the rich man and Lazarus, which did not end well for the rich man. This daughter of a land agent wrote this while living through Ireland's Great Famine, for which neglectful and absentee landlords bore grave responsibility.

At the age of thirty-two she married a clergyman six years her junior, who later became Bishop of Derry. She continued writing, as did her husband and daughter, and she was active in many charities supporting people on the edge of society.

Alexander worked from translations of the original Old Irish hymn which were made when the academic discipline of Celtic Studies was still in its infancy, years before the well-known translation into English by the German scholar Kuno Meyer (1858–

1919) was published in 1902. Yet in spite of all these limitations she has captured some of the essence of the original hymn. Her poem was set to music in 1902 by the Irish composer Charles Villiers Stanford (1852–1924). His rendering uses the traditional Irish tunes known as *Saint Patrick* and *Gartan*, adapted for the organ and the style of the time.

The original prayer was composed as one of a series of *loricae*, breastplates, prayers that use the image of Saint Paul's Letter to the Ephesians (6:14), which in turn draws on older works like the Deuterocanonical Wisdom of Solomon (5:18). The breastplate as a physical protection for a warrior was as familiar an image in ninth-century Ireland as in biblical times. These prayers are cries for protection, and may be especially concerned with the dangers of travel, and physical and spiritual enemies. The breastplate of Ephesians invokes the protection of being 'right' with God, and thus able to repel evil.

The prayer starts with the Trinity, at the start of the day. The opening verb, *Atom riug,* can have two separate meanings, and here can be equally translated as 'I arise' and 'I put on'. Whichever is used, the Trinity is placed centre of the speaker's life, as protection for the day. It is the prayer of the individual, couched in 'I', the human reciter acknowledging the nature of God, asking God's guidance.

After the threefold Trinity, comes a confession of faith in the life, death and resurrection of Jesus, and the raising of the body on the last day. Help is then invoked from other created beings, covering the angels, the heavenly messengers in their various ranks, followed by the Communion of Saints – those who have died and are in happiness in heaven but are still concerned for the peoples of the earth.

The natural world created by God comes next, in all its known forms. Then the hymn becomes personal in its supplication, that the attributes of God will protect the speaker. The dangers are listed, with sin and supernatural adversaries named along with the physical enemies of ninth-century Ireland, where violence could come from natives or Norsemen. Alexander struggles with her text, and tries to bring fears of idolatry and pagandom into relevance for her own world. She also sidesteps another issue, for the Old Irish prayer seeks protection against the spells of women, blacksmiths and druids. The druids, as wizards, remain, but the blacksmiths, with all their mythic attributes, and the women, whether generic or particular, have not been included, though they must have been named in the translations available to Alexander. As with the more violent verses of the psalms, silent deletion has been the preferred option by a woman who conformed to the norms of her society but not at the expense of her half of the human race.

Then, with a change of metre and tune, come the verses involving Christ present in every aspect of life, a part of the hymn that was later reworked and put to the Hebridean tune *Bunessan*.

Finally, the hymn, like the poem on which it is based, returns to the primary statement, of rising today in the name of the Trinity.

The Old Irish text has a prose introduction, which was added later, which places the prayer in the time of Saint Patrick over three centuries earlier, to honour Ireland's greatest saint. This introduction says that the poem was sung by Saint Patrick, who was on his way to the High King at Tara, and gained foreknowledge that his enemies intended to ambush him. To their eyes, Patrick and his followers appeared as deer, an account that gave the prayer the name 'The Deer's Cry'.

The prayer itself has been retranslated several times, but the most poignant version remains that of Kuno Meyer, who taught Celtic Studies in Liverpool and made many deeply moving translations from Old Irish into English. He may have needed this prayer himself, for, as an outspoken supporter of Germany in 1914, he was dismissed from his post.

Before that, one of his students and a fellow-poet, an Irish Nationalist member of the Church of Ireland, Eleanor Hull, had versified another similar hymn in translation, which we sing to another modified traditional tune as *Be Thou my vision*. During the thirty-year 'Troubles', this was a hymn that everyone in Northern Ireland could sing. 'I bind unto myself today' has also been an unexpected gift to our century.

The work of many people, mainly unknown, the prayer in Irish could easily have been lost entirely, or known only to the few who study Old Irish. It has been brought back to light and life by the rendering by Kuno Meyer, and others since, who have improved on it as understanding of the original language became clearer. The fact that Cecil Frances Alexander worked earlier than Meyer, without his language knowledge and from imperfect translations, does not diminish the joy for those who sing her version, and in doing so recreate something that rings true for our age. For some, imagining monks of Columba's monastery reciting in their own language a 'breastplate', especially before a journey, is the key to entering the poem; while for others the words speak to their own times; while for others still, the singing is a spiritual experience as the words of Alexander are rendered in the adapted folk melodies of Stanford. For others, who lived through the Troubles a century after Alexander's hymn was written, it is something that crossed all divides.

> If we cannot as yet think alike in all things, at least we may love alike. Herein we cannot possibly do amiss. For of one point no one can doubt a moment: God is love, and he that dwelleth in love, dwelleth in God, and God in him ... So as far as we can, let us always rejoice to strengthen each other's hand in God.
>
> John Wesley, Letter to a Roman Catholic, written in Ireland, 1749

I arise today
Through a mighty strength, the invocation of the Trinity,
Through belief in the threeness,
Through confession of the oneness
Of the Creator of Creation.

I arise today
Through the strength of Christ's birth with His baptism,
Through the strength of His crucifixion with His burial,
Through the strength of His resurrection with His ascension,
Through the strength of His descent for the judgement of Doom.

I arise today
Through the strength of the love of the Cherubim,
In the obedience of angels,
In the service of archangels,
In the hope of the resurrection to meet with reward,
In the prayers of patriarchs,
In prediction of prophets,
In preaching of apostles,
In faith of confessors,

In innocence of holy virgins,
In deeds of righteous men.

I arise today
Through the strength of heaven;
Light of sun,
Radiance of moon,
Splendour of fire,
Speed of lightning,
Swiftness of wind,
Depth of sea,
Stability of earth,
Firmness of rock.

I arise today
Through God's strength to pilot me:
God's might to uphold me,
God's wisdom to guide me,
God's eye to look before me,
God's ear to hear me,
God's word to speak for me,
God's hand to guard me,
God's way to lie before me,
God's shield to protect me,
God's host to save me,

From snares of devils,
From temptation of vices,
From every one who shall wish me ill,
Afar and anear,
Alone and in a multitude.

I summon today all these powers between me and those evils,
Against every cruel merciless power that may oppose
my body and soul,
Against incantations of false prophets,
Against black laws of pagandom,
Against false laws of heretics,
Against craft of idolatry,
Against spells of women and smiths and wizards,
Against every knowledge that corrupts man's body and soul.

Christ to shield me today,
Against poison, against burning,
Against drowning, against wounding,
So there may come to me abundance of reward.

Christ with me, Christ before me, Christ behind me,
Christ in me, Christ beneath me, Christ above me,
Christ on my right, Christ on my left,
Christ when I lie down, Christ when I sit down, Christ when I arise,
Christ in the heart of every man who thinks of me,
Christ in the mouth of every one who speaks of me,
Christ in every eye that sees me,
Christ in every ear that hears me.

I arise today
Through a mighty strength, the invocation of the Trinity,
Through belief in the threeness,
Through confession of the oneness
Of the Creator of Creation.

Old Irish hymn, translated by Kuno Meyer

THE RAVENSBRÜCK PRAYER

Remember, Lord, not only the men and women of goodwill but also those of ill will. But do not only remember all the suffering they have inflicted on us, remember the fruits we bought, thanks to this suffering, our comradeship, our loyalty, our humility, the courage, the generosity, the greatness of heart which has grown out of all this. And when they come to judgement let all the fruits that we have borne be their forgiveness.

Ravensbrück concentration camp north of Berlin was built for women. It held political prisoners, many of them Poles; Jews; Soviet prisoners of war; German 'anti-socials', such as prostitutes, lesbians and petty criminals; Jehovah's Witnesses; and others. Towards the end of the Second World War a small men's camp was built nearby. The women were used as industrial slave labour, or for pseudo-medical experiments, though a few of the weaker ones were allowed to work by knitting socks for the German Army. All the prisoners had to stand for hours for roll call, were starved and beaten, and slept short hours in flea-bitten dormitories. Many died of starvation and illness; while others were transported and gassed. There were some heroes: many of the Soviet women survived because of one woman who advised them and kept up their morale without the authorities ever discovering who she was. The worse barracks were those of the 'anti-socials', which were the least internally organised by the prisoners themselves and where there was no common faith or political ideology to hold the inmates to a common commitment. Yet in one of them, according to a recent book about the camp, a strongly-built prostitute with a specialist background in sadomasochism not only proved a protective leader where she could, but went to the gas chambers for refusing to beat other prisoners.[3] To many Christians the camp is where the middle-aged watchmaker Corrie ten Boom was held with her sister Betsie after they were arrested for harbouring Jews during the Nazi occupation of the Netherlands. Corrie later wrote about their experience and worked extensively for reconciliation. Betsie, who died there, seems to have achieved a high level of union with God, and the Ravensbrück prayer is associated in many minds with her. It is sometimes said to have been found beside a dead child.

The prayer is anonymous. It first appears in the 1970s, and may be based on writings of Polish prisoners held at Ravensbrück. Whatever the sources, an unknown person was drawn to compress them into this brief, powerful and for many of us hard-to-say prayer, a prayer of forgiveness and the charity that heals the world. This is not an Iona prayer but speaks to the yearning for God, and the tough road we walk with Christ towards the peace through mercy that the island inspires.

Yad Vashem

Outside the Holocaust Museum at Yad Vashem, Jerusalem, a large outdoor sculpture by Nandor Glid commemorates the dead.

We did not find you
in the bazaar
on the Way of the Cross
so we bought bright baubles
and carried carved camels.

Our ersatz experience
cost thirty pieces.

> Then we came to a place
> where skeletal forms
> stretched starkly under a livid sky.
> Backs arched
> in one continual agony
> over the twisted iron limbs;
> fingers spread like giant thorns
> pushing us away;
> skulls screamed silently
> accusing us
> who were not there when it happened –
> or were we?

It was this –
this metal monument of death
which pierced our apathy
and brought us back to life again.
We shed our tears then burning
with shame and grief.

> And we found you there –
> weeping with us.

Margaret Connor

PART TWO – A CLOISTER PILGRIMAGE

Pilgrimage is primarily a state of mind usually expressed through the body. This section concerns a 'route' based on the carvings in the abbey cloisters; and may be undertaken alone, or with two or three others. It involves stillness, the individual entering contemplation through memories evoked by the carvings. There is no need to complete it in one go: it can be picked up at a later time, or at home using the photographs in the book by Ewan Mathers *The Cloisters of Iona Abbey* (Wild Goose Publications), which reproduces each image in black-and-white, accompanied by poetry and notes that give biblical and other references.

The cloister square with its covered walk open on the inside to the central garden is where monks once walked, in reflection and recreation. It was also the place where they could, in the warmer months, study, write with the benefit of natural light, and undertake other craftwork. Though often busy with visitors today, the cloisters can still be a place for quiet meditation, especially out of hours. As an alternative to an outside pilgrimage, the cloisters can provide for the inner journey to unfold.

The cloister pillars were in place when the images were carved, so this is where they were made and where they were intended to be seen. To complement them, this pilgrimage takes in aspects of the medieval buildings met on the circuit, and also the central *Descent of the Spirit*, reflected on in pages 53–57. Around the walls have been placed the tombstones of the late medieval magnates of the Hebrides, people who were significant in their own time, and hopefully loved, but whose names have been forgotten. The images of swords and ships and the abstract decoration call to mind the many people who have come to Iona seeking peace in life, and in death, and the craft of those called to commemorate them. We may find new harmonies between ancient and modern.

The central garden was intended to give pleasure. It is today visited by birds and insects, in greater number by the pollinators in the past when these central gardens might grow medicinal herbs. Many monks and nuns became skilful healers, and cuttings would often be taken from one community to the next, extending knowledge of their uses. Descendants of the plants were said to be found on the island for some three centuries after the Reformation drew monastic life to a close. Part of the journey may involve exploring, in a time of climate crisis and recurring pandemic, the self-sufficiency of our ancestors, and their skill in extracting uses, for food, medicine, bedding and more, from the natural resources among which they lived.

This pilgrimage takes the carvings in the same order as in Mathers' book, with additions to reflect on other features. The cloisters complete a circle of thought, whether in person or in memory. Mathers relates this to the medieval labyrinth, a journey in a single circular pattern. We can take the cloister walk as a journey inward to find God at the heart; and then out again to seek God's life in 'the life of the world'.

The work of the carver, in stone or wood, is to seek out the image from within, pruning away the superfluous. The craftsman has to be attuned to the material being worked, and must allow the image to emerge from the recesses of the soul, and find its form in the material. But art goes beyond the conscious intention of the artist, and speaks to others as well as the self. These images, we may find in pondering them, touch our own souls and experience. They may perhaps make new connections for us between different parts of that experience – and these in turn are touched and renewed by the life of God we meet in scripture, as it is read, heard and lived through each other.

Only two full arches of the original cloister arcade have survived, at the south-west corner. They show the elegant slender pillars that held up the roof, the miniature carved capitals, and their worn foliage. They were the basis for the carvings by the principal carver, Chris Hall, who, over thirty years, drew from the heads of the rough-grained red replacement pillars a range of images relating to the natural world, to the scriptures and to our own round of work, worship and wonder. Some of the carvings on the north arcade were undertaken by a second carver, Douglas Bissett. Each took their main inspiration from the medieval pillars, one with rounded foliage, and the other with a fluted design that draws the eye upwards. As workers co-operating on a common project, their differing styles influenced each other. The carvings are on the inside of the columns, and even so are showing signs of rapid weathering, and perhaps in part in consequence of human touch. Most were carved in the late 1960s and 1970s, and the majority were sponsored, so they carry a reminder for us of those who loved this place before us, and left a memorial to those important in their lives.

Carving takes time, and so does the experience of looking at the work, allowing it to unfold within ourselves. Because these carvings are a sequence, the time we allow ourselves may help us to make new connections. If any one of these carvings speaks to the pilgrim, it is worth staying with it, reflecting on the memories it raises, and either the biblical imagery or the personal imagery that rises in the mind. Only move on when it is time to do so.

For example, the carving I stay with on the east side of the cloister is often the anemone, because it was on a hillside covered in these flowers at the age of six that I first experienced the presence of the God of delight. On the south, church, side of the cloister, the osprey is where I also often linger, having had a close encounter with this huge, fierce-featured bird in recent times.

***

There is no plant in the ground
But is full of God's virtue,
There is no form in the strand
But is full of his blessing.
There is no life in the sea,
There is no creature in the river,
There is naught in the firmament
But proclaims God's goodness.
There is no bird on the wing,
There is no star in the sky,
There is nothing beneath the sun
But proclaims God's goodness.[1]

From Carmina Gadelica

THE EAST SIDE

We start in the north-east corner and travel along the east range of the cloisters (page 17 onwards for images and page 145 onwards for notes in Mathers' book), pausing at each pillar to consider the carvings on the head of the pillar, the capital.

We see on the corner pillar a youthful head with long hair, some of it free and windblown, some of it flowing out of sight into the cloister. This recalls the Spirit moving on the waters at the start of time, Alpha and Omega, the Godhead from which both male and female came into being. We see an image of the wild, creative Spirit who is the same Spirit we meet on Iona through the ordered design on the high crosses, and through the interlace that marks out a boundary to sacred space and prevents the free entrance of evil. An interlace pattern can be seen below the head, for these protective boundaries are themselves part of the creation that the breath of the Spirit calls into being. As yet the lips are closed: the Word is not yet speaking.

***

The grace of the Spirit be with us,
our lives be true in our faith,
that we follow the pattern of the saints,
take our place in the house of the Lord.

May we seek the eternal Trinity,
may our hope be in following Christ,
may we serve the poor in their hardship,
and walk in the will of the Lord.[2]

There follow flowers of the Holy Land as we move southwards, flowers which in ancient times may have been grown on Iona, or were understood through their northerly equivalents. They appear here, on the east, dawn side of the cloisters, as preparation for the story of the Incarnation.

The first is the *thorn*, reminiscent of the crown Christ was to wear. The Creation is immediately followed by an image of its cost. Redemption comes through God addressing the ordinary things of life and taking us with Christ into the extraordinary. Jesus on earth lived life to the full, putting aside any kingship other than the kingship of service and sacrifice that comes from the life within, which depends on no external wealth of possessions, nor on our innate talents or our place in the world. Jesus in the scriptures drew out the good, wherever it was hidden, in the darkest places, even on the cross. This may be a place to consider any deep hurts that have come to the surface while on Iona, hurts that may need to be named, and journeyed with on this pilgrimage. The thorns are entwined, with no visible beginning or end, in an ongoing circle around the pillar, but our perception of them and the place our pain occupies in the circle may change as we continue. The thorn-tree has leaves: it is not dead or barren, but alive, growing.

Next comes the *oak*. After Christ comes Saint Columba. Oak leaves are found throughout the medieval abbey, for the chief architect of the fifteenth-century work came from a Derry family, and the name of this ancient Irish port means 'oak-grove'. It was the site of one of the great monasteries associated with Saint Columba and, we are told in his biography, a place where angels were seen.

The slow-growing and wide-spreading oak is found across

Europe and the Middle East, prized in hot countries for its shade, and everywhere for the strength of the wood, which was used for buildings and boats, and for firewood. While it grows, perhaps for a thousand years, a wide variety of creatures live in, on and under this tree. The oak-apple is present in the image, and from oak galls, round growths in which certain wasps lay their larvae, came ink used to write manuscripts.

The *darnel* reminds that nothing in this life is ever unmixed. Growing in fields of grain, and looking like wheat when young, its seeds can become infected and poisonous. Jesus has a parable of a farmer whose field was found to contain both, but told his labourers not to uproot the darnel but to leave it until harvest, lest the good wheat be damaged. 'Evil and good stand thick around/In the fields of charity and sin/Where we shall lead our harvest in' says Edwin Muir in his poem 'One Foot in Eden'.[3] Humans carry the mix of wheat and darnel within, that which nurtures and that which infects: in Judas they grew when he was on the road with Jesus and his companions. At the Last Supper they shared the wheaten bread and the cup of wine, then he left to betray his friend, and the other men ran away when trouble struck, leaving the women who had walked with them from Galilee to follow Jesus to the Cross.

The next image is the *narcissus*, often called the rose in scripture, and frequently found together with the anemone or lily. The common narcissus, daffodil, with its green leaves followed by the bright yellow trumpet flower, recalls new life in spring.

Also of spring is the smaller *cyclamen* of the next pillar, a member of the primrose family well-known in our climate and which grows wild in the dry soils of the Mediterranean, its broad, waxy leaves contrasting with the delicate flower. It may be the same flower as the Rose of Sharon of the great love-poem the Song of Solomon. This carving was commissioned by the family of a child who died in her sleep while on holiday on Iona. Unknowingly, the artist carved the same number of flowers as her age.

The following *bulrush* brings us to the theme of hope, through the birth of Moses. Matthew's Gospel in particular presents Jesus as a second Moses, chosen by God, escaping death in infancy, leading people to redemption and a new Covenant in a land beyond the wilderness. The artist was inspired by the pointed Gothic arches of the Abbey Church, and spoke of how he was happy to work at carving as part of a tradition, expressing its continuity.

Next comes the *vine*. In the Old Testament, God often refers to the Chosen People as the vine he brought out of Egypt, and Israel as the vineyard that God tends. Jesus is the true vine, of which those who adhere to him are shoots. The fruit makes the wine of the New Covenant offered by Jesus at his last Passover before his violent death, when he says that he will next taste the new wine of the kingdom of heaven. Wine at Passover was for celebration, but in the Greek tradition it also had dark resonances, and in the suffering of Jesus we see this side, in the cost of the redemption desired for all people. Vines are often portrayed with grapes pouring out of chalices in the great Iona work of the late eighth century, the Book of Kells.

Wheat comes next, beside the vine, at the centre of the row, between the thorn at one end and the lily (anemone) at the other. The bread of the Last Supper is central to the Christian tradition. Wheat was the most prized of the grains, especially in northern regions where it needed the better, more sheltered, areas for growth. Whether in the Middle East or on Hebridean islands, wheat was valued for its nutritional content, while barley (and oats in our climate) were used widely as the staple, of lower nutritional value, growing on poorer soils. A grain of wheat that falls to the earth and dies bears much fruit.

Wheat is followed by *vetch*. This is the result of a happy error, for the sculptor had been asked to put darnel here, to continue the themes of joy, new beginnings and their cost. Instead we have a change in the theme, a short turning aside. Some of the family to which vetch belongs, like peas, beans and lentils, are valued food sources; some have been eaten as a food of last resort; some are good for animal forage; and some can poison. Often regarded as a weed, and found on waste ground, vetch supplies bees with nectar and helps them to pollinate.

The tall *palm* is the reminder of the first day of Jesus' last week when he rode into Jerusalem. Palms were waved in celebration and victory, while the trees give shade, and date palms provide sweet fruit. Chris Hall said that this was a hard image to make, to reproduce faithfully the fineness of the fronds in stone.

With the *burning bush* we return to the story of Moses, on what was the artist's favourite capital, for here he felt 'that rare thing among artists and that is inspiration'. God speaks to Moses in the desert, and tells him to go back to Egypt to face and free his own people. Moses, and then the People of Israel, learn that their God is not a national deity limited by borders, but is the One Who Is Who He Is, the free Creator of all place and time. Later, Jesus goes into the desert like Moses, to ponder and seek guidance through fasting and prayer. He returns to preach and free his people, knowing what the cost will be.

The burning bush may at first sight be a deviation from the plant theme, but it is a bush suffused with, on fire with, the presence of God immanent in all Creation, the One glimpsed at rare moments when the humdrum falls away. In these moments we experience for an instant the underlying unity of all things in God, things of heaven and things of earth. The carver included knotwork to connect the story of Moses with the world of Columba, while others have seen in this capital seaweed moving in water, or the act of dancing.

Next comes the *olive*. The fruit of this plant gives oil for healing, for anointing kings and priests, for lighting, and for cooking. It is a plant of peace and the practical values of peace, for the tree lives to a great age and provides shade for humans and other creatures; and wood for carpentry, house-building, utensils and decorative items. The dove returns to Noah's ark carrying an olive branch, showing that the Flood was receding and God was offering healing for the land. In Gethsemane, the garden of the 'olive-press', Jesus goes through his night of terror and betrayal. The healing olive features in key parts of the Book of Kells.

The *fig* is also representative of the Israelites, and of the Hebrew scriptures. This sweet fruit is found in season under the leaves, so has to be searched for. The prophet Micah (4:4) speaks of the time to come when everyone will sit under their own fig-tree and vine. Nathaniel, the 'Israelite without guile', is seen by Jesus sitting under the fig-tree (John 1:48). Zacchaeus, the tax collector of Jericho, climbs a sycamore fig to see Jesus, and gets more joy than he has bargained for (Luke 19:1–9). We also have the strange story of Jesus in his final week cursing a fig-tree that bears no fruit, perhaps a reference to the temple priests bearing in their actions none of the fruits of scripture.

Then comes the *anemone*, the lily of the field, giving a moment of joy amid the suffering of the Passion story. The little flowers come in a range of pastel colours. Jesus said that they do none of the visible work of women, the toiling and the spinning, and yet are arrayed more wonderfully than Solomon in his glory. The Creator provides the work through the aeons that leads to the beauty of these common Mediterranean plants. This carving can also bring to mind the white native anemone of spring woodlands, sometimes called windflower or cowslip.

The first of Chris Hall's carvings, this image also contains, among the stems and flowers, a fish, '*ichthus*', the most ancient Christian symbol. The account of Jesus feeding the five thousand with only a few loaves of bread and a small number of fish is found in all four Gospels. Matthew and Mark have him later feeding another four thousand listeners on the far side of the Sea of Galilee, among the mixed population of Jews and Gentiles. After the Resurrection, Jesus eats fish with his followers to show that he is fully alive and present in the normal activities of life.

The corner image here is of the baptism of Jesus. It may be unexpected that, after the biblical imagery of the plants, we come straight to the start of Jesus' public life. Jesus is shown in the Jordan, the dove of Spirit resting on his hand, with two smaller birds on the land; and John, on the other face of the stone, accompanied by a lively fish, pours water over him. As we had the wind of the Spirit at the beginning of time on the previous corner, here we have the concrete God-made-human. The ultimate Artist enters into the artist's own creation, with the land, the river, the living birds of the air, and the fish with all its connotations.

There is another connection we can make. The corner of mortared stone lying low in the grass of this part of the cloister garth marks the edge of a building older than the Benedictine abbey, which runs under the crossing of the church. Excavated in the 1950s, there are also some burials here. The Benedictine builders incorporated the graves, the 'place of resurrection' of their predecessors, into the medieval cloister. We have at this juncture both baptism into new life and hope of new life in the kingdom of heaven.

Halfway along on this side of the cloister, we have the entrance to the chapterhouse, with its elaborate doorway. Inside are the grand arches with their central pillar which lead to the chapterhouse proper. Here groups can still sit in the places once occupied by the monks as they listened to the daily readings ('chapters') of the Rule of Saint Benedict, and engaged in the business of the community.

The pillar and arches date from around 1210, and the decoration reflects that of the nunnery, except that here everything is more massive, and what was there a double row of ornament has become triple. These great Romanesque arches hold up the roof: it is thought that Iona's famous library was kept in the room above, which is now the current library. A few years after the building of the chapterhouse the new church was extended east, and its floor raised. At the level of the new floor (though now appearing to float in mid-air) this triple pattern of decoration was repeated, but on pointed arches in what was then the newer fashion.

From the Rule of Saint Benedict:

> ... whenever you begin any good work, you must ask of God with the most urgent prayer that it may be brought to completion by God ... for we must at all times use the good gifts that God has placed in us. (From the Prologue)
>
> It is clear that there are four kinds of monk. The first are the Cenobites, that is the 'monastery' kind, who do battle under a Rule and an abbot. The second kind are the Anchorites or Hermits; these are they who are no longer in the first fervour of their religious life but have been tested for a long time in the monastery ... and now, well-equipped to leave the fraternal battle-line for the solitary combat of the desert ... [are] relying on God's aid but now without the support of anyone else. (From Chapter one)

Tools of Good Works (excerpts)

> – In the first place, to love the Lord God with all one's heart, with all one's soul and with all one's strength.
>
> – Then to love one's neighbour as oneself
>
> – To honour all people
>
> – Not to do to another what one would not wish to have done to oneself
>
> – To relieve the poor
>
> – To clothe the naked
>
> – To visit the sick
>
> – To bury the dead

– *To give help in trouble*
– *To console the sorrowful*
– *And never to despair of God's mercy.* (From Chapter four)[4]

The wider world

This may be a good place to reflect on hospitality, which was central to the Benedictine Rule, and on how we offer it, or fail to offer it, today, for those who are refugees on our borders, or homeless within them. The Iona Community prays monthly for a just economic order, and we may add prayer for the hospitality that provides opportunity for all people to see beauty, in the natural world, in the human creative arts, and in all that helps us to grow.

THE SOUTH SIDE

This side of the cloisters is bordered by the church. Churches are usually placed on the north side of the domestic buildings, but here on Iona it is on the south side, meaning that it could be seen by pilgrims from across the Sound and as they disembarked and walked towards it. It also meant that the watercourse, the millstream which runs naturally a little to the north and which served the kitchens and then the washing places and latrines, did not need to be moved. However, in consequence the cloister area is overshadowed and would have been colder than at the nunnery. In both cases, the garden was private to the religious community, part of their home.

The Abbey Church was by contrast open to all, though the nave was the normal place for lay brothers, local people and pilgrims. It was, and is, a place for communal and private prayer, for reflection on faith, worship and healing. Over centuries people have found here shelter, respite, recovery, challenge, acceptance and refreshment.

The carvings alongside this side of the cloisters concern the birds of Iona.

We start with a large, rapid diver, the wide-winged and widespread *gannet*, with its black-tipped wings and yellow patch on its head. Here we have two of them with crossed beaks. This bird visits Iona in stormy weather, but most of the time is at home in the wind and waves. It has excellent eyesight, so can fish even in wild seas, and a strengthened skull, so it can dive at high speed. We speak of children demolishing food rapidly, 'like gannets'.

Another large bird follows, the *osprey*, a summer visitor to the

Highlands and occasionally to Mull, of powerful build and fierce amber eyes, a bird that feeds on fish, entering the water talons first. Monogamous, a pair will return year after year from wintering in Africa, to the same messy nests.

The *snipe* is smaller, slighter, more elegant, a long-beaked freshwater wader. Here, one in the foreground is fishing, plunging into water head first, with great energy, the rushes below giving us the sense of the surface; while another in the background does likewise, and a third is on wing.

The *heron* is known for its stillness, its brooding profile, and its silent flights on huge wings. A solitary creature of river and seashore, sometimes seen on Iona at the machair or the North End, two are depicted here, suggesting that this is a time of mating or of raising young. The heron has a similar profile and the same name in Gaelic (*còrr*) as the sociable crane, which gathers in flocks, a bird that was once widespread in Ireland and is associated with Saint Columba. Once, according to his seventh-century biographer and successor as abbot, Adomnán, Columba welcomed to Iona a storm-weary crane from his homeland in the north of Ireland.

The *dove* is on the central pillar of this side. The biblical references are well-known: the Spirit in the form of the dove appearing as Jesus was baptised, echoing the dove sent forth by Noah from the ark. Here the dove is surrounded by rays of light and power, filling all the space. 'The world is charged with the grandeur of God' wrote the poet Gerard Manley Hopkins.[5] The saint originally known as 'Foxy' in childhood, then Colum, then Colum of the Church, Columcille, was known through a Latin form of his name as Columba, 'dove'. He is honoured here as one filled with the Spirit, as the dove is surrounded by the rays of God's power. Many visitors to Iona will recall that at times a flock of white doves nest in the abbey tower, while wild rock doves sometimes frequent coastal areas, and probably gave their name to Pigeons' Cave on the south-east coast of Iona. The dove is also an emblem of innocence and gentleness, and this carving was partly sponsored by friends of the artist in memory of a deceased child.

The world that is charged with God is also at times a place of terror. The *merlin* and *swallow* on the next pillar show nature in its incompatibilities. The merlin, an occasional visitor to Iona, is one of the smallest birds of prey but well able to catch and feast off other birds in flight, even one as fast as the swallow. Swallows return year after year to the same nest sites on Iona, including Saint Odhràin's Chapel. Psalm 84 tells of the swallow finding a nest for the young in God's temple.

The rare great northern *diver*, or loon, follows, appearing among rushes and seemingly brooding a clutch of eggs. This parental act of protection and care balances the previous image, giving us a fuller sense of the natural world. Solitary males are seen in winter and spring along the east and north coasts of Iona.

The *corncrake* is now another rare bird, but one that is, fortunately, breeding on Iona well, and has spread to the west of Mull and to Staffa. It comes from Africa in April and returns in September. A nondescript brown, land-nesting bird, it is heard more than seen, with the males giving their loud, incessant calling on summer nights. It needs tall grasses in which to hide and lay its eggs. A beetle made by a friend of the carver is also present on this pillar.

The final bird on this side is the *tern*, sometimes called a seaswallow, which feeds by skimming the surface of the waves. One bird is diving towards the water, its wings as elegant as a ballet dancer's arms, while another has its feet on land. Until recently, Arctic terns nested on Eilean Annraidh (Island of Storms) off the north-east tip of Iona, but non-native mink have destroyed the colony.

Then come two smaller arches which have survived the weathering of the years but carry few decorative features. Then come very different images at the corner.

This corner pillar shows a dramatic face with teeth bared, flared nostrils and burial bands falling away. This is Lazarus being raised from the grave, an incident in the life of Jesus where, by giving back life to his friend to complete his earthly journey, Jesus' own fate was sealed. Lazarus is struggling upwards to receive this gift of love: coming fully back to life, as happens to many visitors to Iona, is not always a simple or easy process.

We have moved with the images at the corners of the cloisters from the Spirit brooding over the waters at the beginning of time, to Jesus in the Jordan, God become human, to the reality of death for all humans and our need to confront this journey we all take.

The following reflection is based on the ancient concept of the harrowing of hell, of Jesus bringing back to the fullness of life those who had died before him, and before their time.

***

In the dew after Jesus
tumbled out from the tomb
Jephthah's daughter in the bloom
before womanhood,
called by her name,
and forgave.

Two thieves came like brothers
arms crossing shoulders
one still calling Jesus
by his own, given name.

Sad-hearted Judas
clinging to shadows
slipped out and began
to forgive his own fall.

A wonder of prophets
once slain for the profits
of priests passing by
without comfort;

those killed in the fields or at prayer
from Abel to infants that Herod despised,

like shadows in sunshine
dissolved and reformed,
learning to live
with love without end.

Rosemary Power

Finding a key image on this side, which depicts birds, may involve reflection on movement and travel. The corner now reached is the part of the cloisters most passed through, as people enter through the main doors and make for the nave of the church. It can be a place to reflect on the way in which people move today, as have monks, tourists, pilgrims, historians and others between church and chapterhouse, worship and business; or it may be about the people who pass through our own lives, sometimes only once, leaving something of themselves with us.

The wider world

During the Covid-19 pandemic, we saw the earth struggling to recover in the days when pollution from transport went down, when the silence brought back birdsong and beetles. There was hope that we could live without killing our planet, that we could change our ways of exploitation, and take seriously the reality that our actions impinge on each other. We may need to find the voice to lament, to mourn and seek God's help for our reshaping, within ourselves and across our world. The story of Lazarus and the two sisters who mourned him, Martha the homemaker who made the astonishing act of faith equalled only by Simon Peter, and Mary the disciple and prophet who anointed Jesus before his death, all may be of help in finding this voice of lament and renewal.

***

Our God, our help down all the years,
who walks with us through all our fears,
be present with us now.
Remind us we are not at war
with illness but we need remorse
and tears for hope to grow.

We cannot now with guns or drones
or bombs and bitterness make known
our unease, greed, self-will.
We know of floods, pollution, dearth
through stunted crops on famished earth,
where creatures fall and fail.

Give us lament, the ancient voice
of courage speaking of the choice
we made to go astray;
help us bewail, and cleanse with grief
the cost of trusting self-belief
and making others pay.

In life, in health, through famine, fear,
in isolation, grief, we find
another walks beside;
who never heeds what's wealth's preserve,
but sees the cost and risks that serve
the needs of humankind.

Rosemary Power

THE WEST SIDE

This range of the cloister arcade starts with the other side of death. We have seen Lazarus raised and now on the cornerstone we have new life in the birth of Jesus. Here is a human baby, with a rounded face and haloed head, an arm raised, on one side of the stone, and on the other the fat, kicking legs. With Lazarus we have been raised to life again: now we have the gift of love Incarnate to live with. Jesus 'turns the corner' for us here, with hope for the world and hope for us after this life.

There follows on this side of the cloisters a series of flowers found in Britain and Ireland.

The *primrose*, a small, yellow, spring flower, is short-stemmed, comes up when snow may still be on the ground, can last the summer and can be widespread on grassy banks. Alexander Carmichael commented on its prevalence in children's lives in the Hebrides of the late nineteenth century, and prints a song:

Primrose, primrose
And wood-sorrel,
The children's food
In summer ...[6]

From Carmina Gadelica

Then come two surviving and much-weathered medieval arches on which the modern pillars, arches and carvings are based. They held up the original roof that opened, like the modern one, into the central garden. The first pillar is deeply fluted, but flowering at the top. The second, in a gentler, rounded style, shows flowers with entwined, encircling stems. It appears that they were undertaken by different carvers working together, as part of a communal effort.

Wild rose and *heather* are the next of the modern carvings, entwined around each other as they are often found in the wild. Symbols of Scotland, the rose is also often associated with the Virgin Mary, and the delicately-scented, native, pink wild rose, or dog rose, is especially suited here, where the nunnery and in the later Middle Ages also the abbey were dedicated to Mary. It is not so common on Iona as on the mainland but can occasionally be found in hedgerows. Rosehips were gathered in autumn as a good source of Vitamin C and for the treatment of winter colds. Heather, in its glory in July and August, was used in the past as bedding material, which gave a pleasant and fragrant night, and also to roof houses.

Bog myrtle has a pungent scent. Found on wet moorlands, such as those on Iona, it was used by peat-cutters and others working in these places to ward away midges. Dried, it was used to repel moths from fabrics. There is a folk rhyme in its honour:

> I am plucking thee,
> thou gracious red myrtle,
> in name of the Father of virtues,
> in name of the Son whom I love,
> in name of God's eternal Spirit.
> For virtue of good man,
> for virtue of good span,
> for virtue of good woman,
> for virtue of good life,
> for virtue of good step.

For virtue of good love,
for virtue of good leap,
for virtue of good cause,
for virtue of good life
without peril and without reproach.[7]

From Carmina Gadelica

The *Christmas rose*, or *hellebore*, is not a wild flower but an incomer, sometimes found in gardens on Iona, which again reminds of the birth of Jesus at the darkest time. Here, the carving is full of movement. The deep swirls may look like the way snow can move with the wind. It may carry hints of the second of the medieval carvings, with its curved tendrils, serving to recall that the art of the carver is to discover and bring to light what the stone permits. The artist has to be attuned to the material as well as to the recesses of mind and soul, and sometimes we see, as here, what can be drawn out of the stone, and what influences were at work on the carver.

With the *lily of the valley* the carver reverts to his more familiar style. Again a biblical plant, and one associated with purity of mind, it is not native to the UK but can be found in the wild in some places in Scotland, its broad green leaves opening to display on a single stem the set of small white bells that move together at a slight breeze. Its intense scent makes it known before it is seen.

The *gentian* is a delicate small plant. The field gentian, with a small purple flower, is occasionally found on Iona in late summer and autumn, and prefers ledges with sandy soil, such as those above Sandeels Bay. The spring gentian is a rare and protected species with a vivid blue flower, which prefers open land. It survived the Ice Age in a few places in Britain and Ireland, such as the limestone of the Burren in the west of Ireland.

The *snowdrop* is the first flower to come up in late winter, often through snow, or else through the last year's brown leaf mould, and often creates a carpet in old woodland. Some grow wild near the Heritage Centre. We see here the two larger leaves from a cluster of narrow green leaves at the base supporting a stem with a single, drooping, white bell, all portrayed in a massive style for a small flower. It may have been introduced to our part of the world in recent centuries, a reminder that humans can be responsible for the spread of much that is beautiful, at no cost to what is already there.

Birdsfoot trefoil, sometimes known as eggs and bacon, has a bright yellow flower with small leaves, and grows along grassy roadsides and on the sandy soils of the machair. Here it is depicted in a rather different, bolder and less detailed style than is usual, and even more massively than the snowdrop. The plant was used in the past in animal fodder. Like vetch a member of the pea family, it is visited by bees, butterflies and other insects.

There follows the sweet-smelling *honeysuckle*, a familiar climbing plant, found on sea-cliffs and ledges, which has blooms beloved of bees. Here the new growth shoots out of the old branch, filling the carved area with its complex flowers and leaves, reflecting the patterns of interlace on the older carvings of the monastery.

Butterwort is another small flower more valued in the past than today. In the Hebrides, where it grows in poor, damp soils, it was used as protection against evil; and for the preservation of the essential processed food that fed people throughout the year, butter. Juice from the sticky leaves that trap midges and other small insects was smeared on cows' udders as a protection, and indeed served to heal sores through the bactericide it produces. Butterwort was also used to ferment and thicken milk products.

The *crocus*, sometimes called the sand crocus, is another incomer species from more southerly parts of Europe. Again growing close to the earth with a single flower, it blooms in spring. Here it is shown with the tendrils that spiral as they grow, which can link in the imagination to the spiral art of the pre-Christian period, and to the labyrinth journey that the cloister carvings emulate. The crocus grows on the mound outside the Reilig Odhràin Chapel.

The last plant on this side is *sundew*, whose white flowers open only in warm sunshine. Like the peregrine snatching the swallow from the skies in the south arcade, it is a reminder that we should not over-romanticise nature, for this plant is a fly-catcher, and some of its victims are portrayed on its sticky pads.

The corner pillar gives us two more images. On this, the west side, we see two hands breaking bread. The hands are large, working hands, and the loaf is long and thin, like French bread. Around on the north side is the wine, in the common, shared cup for all to drink from. The base of the cup stands out – we cannot see the hands that tilt it towards the receiver: they must be the hands that also break the bread and are now just out of sight. The head receiving the wine might be African in the wide nose and the short hair worn close to the skull. Humanity from across the world is present on this Hebridean island in the breaking of bread and sharing of wine.

***

This poem is based on the resurrection experiences of Jesus as seen through the lens of the ceasefire in 1994 which led to Northern Ireland's Good Friday Agreement of 1998, after 30 years of 'The Troubles'.

After the ceasefire

After the ceasefire
   Jesus cooked a meal.
The Lord Chief Justice came
   curious, his wife with trepidation.
The fox strutted out of his hole,
   brushed, sleek,
      and found his desires before him:
         Joanna took him in hand.
The son of the father was washed,
   slicked, shocked and supported
      by Martha and Matthew, and met his replacement.

There was a hush when Judas pushed
   the gate and Magdalen moved up.
Simon arrived from manoeuvres,
   dirty red hands carried rounds,
      sisters paid prices, bought spices,

there were children grown bent who went straight
when the doors of the shore were opened
and the wounded came in and sat down.[8]

Rosemary Power

Looking at them from outside, the west range buildings are the most puzzling archaeologically, for there is no evidence of medieval foundations, though it is inconceivable that this side would have been left open to the prevailing wind and rain. Outside, through the modern entrance, is the 'peace garden', which lies at the far end of the Street of the Dead. This was developed within the ruined walls of a medieval baking and brewing house, which is in turn based upon an older building. Just to its north is the herb garden maintained by the Iona Community, with its scents and flowers attracting insects today as in the past.

Again there is the opportunity to stay with one of the carved plants which speaks personally. Alternatively, it may be a time to move outside and look at the living plants.

Before moving to the north side of the cloister, we may look at some older stonework. In the corner beside the shop entrance, set in the wall, is a blocked-up decorated arch. Some of the carvings have been protected from the weather by the later entrance. At one stage, before the shop doorway was built, the blocked-up arch was the grand entrance to the refectory above, the place of common meals, then as it is now.

***

God bless this house from its base to its height
And God bless each lintel, each stone and each board.
God bless the hearth, the table for food,
And God bless each room to give night's peaceful rest.

God bless the door that we open it wide
To the stranger and poor as well as our kin.

God bless the windows that give us the gift
Of the light of the sun, the moon and the stars.

God bless the rafters over our heads
And every strong wall that surrounds us today.

May peace, love and affection remain with our neighbours,
God bless all who live here, keep them from harm,
May God guide us at last to his own kingly home.[9]

The wider world

Both the corner carvings and the archway indicate a place for reflection on hospitality in a world in change, and on the changing climate which cries out for the more fortunate nations to react with hospitality to those fleeing the destruction of their environment, the violence of war and the growth of oppressive regimes.

This is also the place of the bell. A ship's bell was donated to the work of the Iona Community during the period of rebuilding. It has been used to call people to meals, as the bell in the church tower calls people to worship. It may also be a reminder of the bells that held power in the early church to which Columba and his followers belonged. These had practical roles but also a spiritual one in blessing the land in which they were heard.

> *The sweet little bell that is rung on a windy night, I would rather go to meet it than to meet a wanton woman.*[10]
>
> Irish quatrain

THE NORTH SIDE

The north side of the cloister gives us more flowers of Iona, the first eight in a noticeably different style. They were carved by a second craftsman, Douglas Bissett. As he and Chris Hall worked at the same time, they influenced each other.

The first, in a massive but simple design, is the *marguerite*, the ox-eye daisy, found along roadsides, the larger sister of the tiny daisy known to every child, with similar white petals and bright orange-yellow centre. Here it is shown with its serrated leaves. Scotland's best-known Margaret is the eleventh-century queen and saint, who rebuilt the monastery on Iona when it was ruinous. One of the stained-glass windows in the abbey commemorates this English refugee from the Norman conquest. The flute-like form of the carving echoes one of the medieval pillars, just as Chris Hall's carvings frequently echo the carving on the other capital.

The next, the tiny ivy-leaved *toadflax*, is given magnified treatment here, perhaps a recognition that large and small, known and unknown, we are all part of God's valued creation. This plant is often found in rock crevices and by footpaths, with its glossy leaves lying low to the ground, and its small purple flowers resembling those of its larger relative the snapdragon. It grows in profusion in the nunnery.

The next is recognisable to many, the *thistle*. Various kinds grow on Iona, where their seed is spread on the wind and in the past also through the dung of the beasts of burden that fed upon them. Thistles are well-known for their purple heads and spiny leaves, and the spear thistle is the national flower of Scotland. The creeping thistle has smaller flowers with a sweet honey-like perfume, and spreads through roots as well as seeds. The marsh thistle also grows on Iona.

Another flower of Scotland is the little white *burnet rose*, depicted next and given equal treatment to its larger fellow, the thistle. It is creamy white, with a strong, sweet perfume and grows on rocky ledges by the sea, especially above Traigh Mhòr. We return here to the rounded form favoured in Chris Hall's style and echoing that of the first of the medieval pillars.

The *dandelion* grows everywhere. Its seed-heads have been enjoyed by generations of children as they blow the dandelion clocks. The leaves can be used in salads and as a diuretic, while the roots, though also bitter-tasting, have been roasted and ground to use as foodstuff, most noticeably as a coffee substitute in times of hardship, like the Second World War. We return to the fluted style for this carving.

Navelwort, or *wall pennywort*, used to be found growing along the walls of the nunnery and prefers damp and shady places, along the coast and on mossy roofs. Its green-pink flowers are like those of the snapdragon but smaller. They grow on a stem above a rosette of broad green leaves with a depression in the centre that was thought to resemble the navel. It had various medicinal uses in the past.

The *foxglove* is one of the fairy flowers in Gaelic tradition. Not common on Iona but found growing in profusion across the Highlands and Islands, in particular around abandoned crofts, this tall plant has many purple, or sometimes white, bell-like flowers hanging from a single stem. It sways with the wind, as this carving displays. A poisonous plant, its extract has been used medicinally for heart disease.

The *iris*, or *yellow flag*, is widespread on the island and is distinctive for its tall leaves and large yellow June flower. The root was sometimes used in the Hebrides for black dye or to make ink. This carving was unfinished when Douglas Bissett died, and may remind us of all unfinished work that is yet pleasing to God.

The *harebell*, or *Scottish bluebell*, is a delicate summer plant of heaths, machair and dry acid land, with small, open blue bells. Now a protected species, this plant is again associated with the fairies in folk tradition, as is its namesake the hare.

Tormentil, one of the cinquefoils, with its five-sectioned leaves and small yellow flowers, is here displayed with four petals. It was used medicinally to treat intestinal disorders, and the roots were used traditionally in the Hebrides for tanning fishing nets and shoe-leather. It is common on light soil and moorlands, flowers from spring to autumn, and it is one of the first plants to regrow on burnt moorland.

Another small plant with solitary flowers, in this case white-petalled, is the *sea campion*, which grows on rocks and shingle by the sea. It has a bladder-like calyx that supports the flower during high tides. One of the small flowers that many of us do not notice in the course of modern life, or do not give a name to, it often forms mats of grey-green waxy foliage, and is found along the north-west coasts of Europe.

Saxifrage, though another small plant, is the 'stonebreaker', as its name, derived from Latin, implies. It grows in cracks and between the stones of walls, appearing to pull them apart. Perhaps it can bring to mind the prophet Ezekiel's words that God wants to take away the heart of stone and give us back a heart of flesh, so that we can feel and love again. On Iona, the golden saxifrage, a low-growing plant in damp places, is present.

The corner will bring us back to the beginning and the Alpha and Omega figure of the Spirit moving on the face of the waters. We have first, on the north side of the cornerstone, in contrast to the immensity of the Spirit whom we seek, an image from the Gospels which gives us a starting point in the small and concrete. This connection is made through another plant, the *mustard seed*.

Jesus, like the nearby image of the Spirit with which we started, has long flowing hair which forms flowers or leaves at its ends, a reminder that he like them will die. He holds the seed between his fingers and preaches against a backdrop of mountains, which are rounded like those of Mull across the Sound of Iona. Jesus told his disciples (Matthew 17:20) that if they had faith the size of a mustard seed they would be able to move mountains.

There are also his stories:

> He told them another parable: 'The kingdom of heaven is like a mustard seed, which a man took and planted in his field. Though it is the smallest of all seeds, yet when it grows, it is the largest of garden plants and becomes a tree, so that the birds come and perch in its branches.'
>
> Matthew 13:31–32 (NIV UK)

The parable makes the link for us between the plants of three sides of the cloister and the birds of the church side. It is followed by a complementary parable in verse 33: 'The kingdom of heaven is like yeast that a woman took and mixed into about thirty kilograms of flour until it worked all through the dough.' This links us to the bread of the last, north-west, corner pillar, and perhaps also to the woman held in the canopy of creation by the dove in the central work of the art.

We have come full circle, returning to the place from which we started, where the Spirit moves on the face of the waters. In our ends are our beginnings. This may be a time to return to any image that connected deeply, to allow it to open up to the onlooker.

Time may be needed to reflect on what has brought each pilgrim to this place, and the interactions and conversations that have occurred. There is a seat in the cloisters, with the words carved on its back: Be Still. 'Be still and know that I am God' says Psalm 46, verse 10.

***

In the time of Covid-19

The urban friend of friend who wished,
though skilled in academe and Internet,
to be when outside less
outside recovered knowledge
said, yearning to learn again:

'I can't join in enjoying
the weeds between the cracks
of walls and pavements and
our enforced time to look.'

But did you never
blow a dandelion
to tell the time;
chew honey from clover;

make a daisy chain;
yellow the chin with buttercup
to gauge your preference;
dance with a poppy;
have a brush with a nettle;
prick yourself on thistles;
scratch yourself on brambles –
and eat the fruit the birds left;

see bindweed and buddleia
along the railway lines,
or ivy creep
up boarded windows?

Did you bus through hills
heathered and brackened;
see may spring white
beside the motorway?

Did you harvest conkers in the park,
see red of rowan, elder's purple;
or watch the slender silver
of a wind-swayed birch?

Is it now so vast a task
to trust forgotten knowledge,
one foot in Eden, name
the vetch or celandine,
columbine, cuckoo-pint,
groundsel, forget-me-not?

Do we need to stoop again

with the close eyes of childhood,
lest we close our minds against
both neighbouring death
and greening earth;

bees feeding through flowers,
beetles below them,
birds above them;
and the stars above us all?

Rosemary Power

The wider world

After following the carvings, the pilgrim can return to the entrance to the central garden. Here is the statue of the *Descent of the Spirit*. This was placed here before the carvings were made and may be understood in relation to them, and as an international, and interfaith, expression of the times since the abbey was rebuilt. For a reflection on this work see pages 53–57.

***

God of the elements, Ancient of Days,
you gave us the land to feed and delight us;

Wind of the Spirit, bringer of growth,
you gave us each other to reach and restore us;

Jesus the carpenter, human in weakness,
you gave us our labour, to cherish your kingdom.

Bless us, restore us, stretch us to serve you,
Friend of all need, give us starlight to guide us,

on the road to your home with the people you love.

Rosemary Power

Postscript

Missing to many eyes is the fuchsia, so prominent in Iona's hedgerows, whose drooping flowers, usually bright red, were unknown to the medieval monks, for it comes from South America and was used at first for hedgerows here in the eighteenth century. In Irish its name is *deoraí Dé*, the tears of God.

The carvings inside the abbey, many of them from the fifteenth century, can yield much to reflect on. The twentieth-century stained-glass windows help us not only to recall the saints they depict but to look at the way in which sunlight, at different times of the day and the year, gives different effects.

There are other sculptures on Iona, most noticeably the modern *Fallen Christ* by the artist Ronald Rae, placed in February 2008 beside the MacLeod Centre, a short walk for the more robust. It is found through the gate by the Iona Community bookshop, up a short hill on a road that cuts through the vallum, the ditch-and-dyke boundary to the sacred central space, and to the left of the entrance to the MacLeod Centre.

PART THREE – PILGRIMAGE BY BOAT

Pilgrimage is a big part of the story of Iona today, through the arriving and the departing, and in our communal and solitary activities on the island. Of these, the most long-standing is the weekly walk led by staff of the Iona Community's island centres. Others do this journey in their own groups, and a guide by Jane Bentley and Neil Paynter (*Around a Thin Place*, Wild Goose Publications) gives a route and suggestions for reflection and prayer. *Iona: A map*, drawn by Diarmid, is helpful for both land and water journeys.

The following route is by boat around the island, and is envisaged as a group experience, undertaken with the sound and movement of the waves and wind, and the sights of the island, the art of the natural world the focus. This pilgrimage contains suggestions for communal prayer and reflection, and some groups may wish to bring songs with them to mark the stopping-places.

* Note: This is not something that can be undertaken alone: it requires the skills of an experienced local boatman who knows the tides, dangerous currents and other features of the coastline. A list of such people is kept on the isle of Iona website:

http://www.welcometoiona.com

http://www.welcometoiona.com/visiting-iona/local-businesses/boat-trips/

One of the smaller island boats may be suitable to hire for a group, and people can see the stopping-places of the main pilgrimage, other than Loch Staonaig and the Hermit's Cell, and also several not seen by walkers. To reiterate, this is not something to be done alone, as the currents are dangerous, and travel in single-person vessels can be perilous.

The route is conceived as going southwards from the jetty, that is, clockwise round the island, though it may be necessary to undertake the pilgrimage in reverse if the wind is unfavourable. In consequence, the different points of interest and reflection have been numbered, so that the pilgrimage can be undertaken the other way round. This means starting with the first point, the jetty, then turning to the fifteenth point, the Nunnery, and taking the points in reverse order, but following the second point with the sixteenth, 'Back to the jetty'.

Before starting it is suggested that people bring with them two pebbles from the shore.

1. THE JETTY

This has been a landing place for centuries, for pilgrims and island residents, and is now the pier for thousands of visitors each summer. This is where we arrive with our luggage, the visible and the internal; and where we leave from.

Psalm 84 is one of the pilgrim songs of people on their way to Jerusalem and the temple.

> How lovely is your dwelling-place,
>   LORD Almighty!
> My soul yearns, even faints,
>   for the courts of the LORD;
> my heart and my flesh cry out
>   for the living God.
> Even the sparrow has found a home,
>   and the swallow a nest for herself,

>   where she may have her young –
> a place near your altar,
>   Lord Almighty, my King and my God.
> Blessed are those who dwell in your house;
>   they are ever praising you.
>
> Blessed are those whose strength is in you,
>   whose hearts are set on pilgrimage.
> As they pass through the Valley of Baka,
>   they make it a place of springs;
>   the autumn rains also cover it with pools.
> They go from strength to strength,
>   till each appears before God in Zion.
>
> Hear my prayer, Lord God Almighty;
>   listen to me, God of Jacob.
> Look on our shield, O God;
>   look with favour on your anointed one.
>
> Better is one day in your courts
>   than a thousand elsewhere;
> I would rather be a doorkeeper in the house of my God
>   than dwell in the tents of the wicked.
> For the Lord God is a sun and shield;
>   the Lord bestows favour and honour;
> no good thing does he withhold
>   from those whose way of life is blameless.
>
> Lord Almighty,
>   blessed is the one who trusts in you.

Psalm 84 (NIV UK)

We reflect on those

– coming from curiosity
– arriving after years of waiting
– returning
– holiday-making
– searching.

We ask that they may

– find here the peace that lies within
– find prayer *'where prayer has been valid'*
– enrich the island with their presence
– leave refreshed.

***

Give me my scallop shell of quiet,
My staff of faith to walk upon,
My scrip of joy, immortal diet,
My bottle of salvation,
My gown of glory, hope's true gage,
And thus I'll take my pilgrimage …

Walter Raleigh (c. 1552–1618)

2. MARTYRS' BAY

This was another key landing place, and the ancient road that started here passes through the village, goes past the Saint Ronan's Chapel beside the nunnery, and on towards the abbey, entering the precincts just after the west door of the Reilig Odhràin Chapel, where it is uncovered and known as the 'Street of the Dead'. There were once a number of high crosses along this path, the last of which is the Saint Martin's Cross, where the walking pilgrimage starts today. (The imagery carved on Saint Martin's Cross is considered on pages 17–28.)

It was at this bay that in earlier times the bodies of the dead were brought to shore for burial on Iona. In the field beyond the bay is a mound, *An Ealadh*, where the archaeologist Richard Reece found evidence of an early Christian burial ground, apparently of women who had never had children, an indication that this might have been the site of a nunnery, a consideration revisited by Kathryn Forsyth recently.

The usual view is that the name Martyrs' Bay is translated directly from Gaelic and, as the loanword from Greek meant 'witness' to Christ, it was where the dead were brought to this 'Bay of the Witnesses'. The Christian dead, however they died, had, it was hoped, witnessed to Christ in their lives.

Those buried on the island in ancient times and later include those who died in age, or by drowning, or childbirth, or illness. We know that in 664, 683 and 700 there were plagues which affected Iona. The loss of people to harvest the crops meant that the famine that followed was the regular companion of widespread illness.

Reminders of youthful death are found here. On the shore

stands the island's war memorial, listing the names of those who died in both world wars. We may also recall the untold lives, of the poor, of those who died before their time, those who were lost at sea, and the bodies of strangers from the sea that were buried on this island.

The Free Church, now a private house, was built after the Disruption, the split within the Church of Scotland in 1843. The major reunion was in 1929, and this became a model for many Christians in the charitable accommodation between those who thought differently on many issues but were united in their core beliefs.

We recall, as we give thanks for the world around us, those things that are not right in our lives and the life of the world, all those things that affect others and mar our journey. We pray for those who seek to relieve the slavery of international debt and unjust structures that deny the fullness of life to our neighbours. We recall those who lay down their lives for others; and all of us who have no idea what God may ask, and how we will respond. We recall those who worked, died, lost their health in consequence of our own plague, Covid-19.

> They went to a place called Gethsemane, and Jesus said to his disciples, 'Sit here while I pray.' He took Peter, James and John along with him, and he began to be deeply distressed and troubled. 'My soul is overwhelmed with sorrow to the point of death,' he said to them. 'Stay here and keep watch.'
>
> Going a little farther, he fell to the ground and prayed that if possible the hour might pass from him. 'Abba, Father,' he said, 'everything is possible for you. Take this cup from me. Yet not what I will, but what you will.'
>
> Mark 14:32–36 (NIV UK)

***

My Lord God,
I have no idea where I am going.
I do not see the road ahead of me.
I cannot know for certain where it will end.
Nor do I really know myself,
and the fact that I think that I am following your will
does not mean that I am actually doing so.
But I believe that the desire to please you
does in fact please you.
And I hope I have that desire in all that I am doing.
I hope that I will never do anything apart from that desire.

And I know that, if I do this, you will lead me by the right road
though I may know nothing about it.
Therefore will I trust you always though
I may seem to be lost and in the shadow of death.

I will not fear, for you are ever with me,
and you will never leave me to face my perils alone.

Thomas Merton (1915–1968)[1]

3. ALONG THE COAST

The coast here is rocky, with small bays of golden sands. Before the road turns inland, into the central valley, we see on the shore a large pink boulder. Known locally as the Pulpit Rock, this glacial erratic was brought during an Ice Age from neighbouring Mull. It reminds us of the ancient nature of the rocks beneath our feet, and the vast length of time in which God prepared this earth for our comfort, sustenance and curiosity.

Near here the monks of Iona may have had a fish-trap, a means of working communally to feed a large number of people. These traps are usually made as funnels, of wicker or similar materials, placed from the shore out to sea at a strategic place, into which at high tide the sea washes fish (and some marine mammals, such as seals). At low tide these can be harvested or returned to the sea.

We pass Traigh Mhòr, the Big Strand, at the end of which is the small Traigh nan Siolag, Sandeels Bay.

4. SANDEELS BAY

This bay was part of the economic life of the island for many years, as sandeels provided bait for fishermen, which in turn allowed households to add to their diet. Seaweed was gathered in bays like this for use as fertiliser on the land. There is another Sandeels Bay opposite on Mull.

'Economy' comes from the Greek word for the home, which also gives the word ecumenical. The Oxford Dictionary defines economy as a modern term for the 'managements of the concerns and resources of a community'.

We have prayed on this island and across the world for a just and sustainable use of our finite resources, that the needs of the many may be met, and not at the cost of greed. Perhaps we have kept the concerns and the resources of a society as separate issues. But with the climate crisis upon us, and the aftermath of the Covid-19 pandemic, we are forced to consider the issues we have hidden. The resources of our household of this planet, which we have been called to steward for the good of all, are on the brink of collapse. Yet there is still time for us to consider future generations and our duty towards them.

> 'Come, all you who are thirsty,
>   come to the waters;
> and you who have no money,
>   come, buy and eat!
> Come, buy wine and milk
>   without money and without cost.
> Why spend money on what is not bread,
>   and your labour on what does not satisfy?
> Listen, listen to me, and eat what is good,
>   and you will delight in the richest of fare.
> Give ear and come to me;
>   listen, that you may live.
> I will make an everlasting covenant with you,
>   my faithful love promised to David ...'
>
> Isaiah 55:1–3 (NIV UK)

Here we reflect on what land, sea and shore provide for us; and the just stewardship of all, as we pass this place where people both took what they needed, and left behind, so that the future resources would be renewed. May we turn from non-renewable sources of food and energy as we work to protect the planet.

***

Bread broken

O Christ,
    does a mother stop
    from stooping and sifting the rubbish
    in a South American rubbish tip –
    stop and listen to the songbird
    and know the pain, which pierces her heart,
    is your pain?

O Christ,
    does a child stop
    from hustling and haggling the punters
    on the pavements of Brazil –
    stop and look at the stars
    and know that the hunger in his belly
    is your hunger?

O Christ,
    does a young girl stop
    from walking and working the streets
    in the suburbs of our cities –
    stop and enjoy the scent of a flower
    and know that the anger in her heart
    is your anger?

O Christ,
> does an old man stop
> from carrying and cursing water,
> in the polluted wastes of Iraq –
> stop and feel the wind on his face
> and know that his thirst
> is your thirst?
>
> God, your presence breaks into our world.
> Christ, your pain breaks the shell of our understanding.
> Holy Spirit, you are at one with the world's suffering,
> Be present at your table
> as we share with the poor of the world,
> Christ's body broken for the life of the world.
>
> *Kate McIlhagga*[2]

5. THE MARBLE QUARRY

The coast has become rocky as we move southwards.

At our last reflection we considered our dependence on the provision of food and other goods from the natural world. Here at the place where the boats for the marble quarry loaded up, at this risky, waved-washed landing-place, we consider our industrial heritage.

Our economics are not an end in themselves but a means to ensure the resources to allow our household, our society, to function well for all peoples on earth. The resources are for wise use, for the practical needs of life, for our activities, and for those things which help us grow and nourish our souls; so that what we need, what we desire, and what is for beauty do not cost the earth.

The green marble of Iona was created under heat and great pressure in the earth. Iona marble has given delight across the world, and the last major pieces taken from this quarry form the panels of the Communion table of the restored Iona Abbey. This replaced the medieval one, which is also believed to have been of Iona marble, which had disappeared slowly after the Reformation, when visitors took away small pieces. This site with machinery left here in the early twentieth century, when the last attempts to work the site were abandoned, is a Scheduled Ancient Monument, now protected as part of our common heritage of skill. Volunteers have recently repainted the machinery to conserve it.

Here the creativity of God who formed the marble, the use of beauty to draw us to the Creator, the crafts of engineering and of seamanship to load the stone, and the economic skills that found markets across the world, can be celebrated.

> I will rejoice over Jerusalem
>   and take delight in my people;
> the sound of weeping and of crying
>   will be heard in it no more.
>
> Never again will there be in it
>   an infant who lives but a few days,
>   or an old man who does not live out his years;
> the one who dies at a hundred
>   will be thought a mere child;
> the one who fails to reach a hundred
>   will be considered accursed.

> They will build houses and dwell in them;
>> they will plant vineyards and eat their fruit.
> No longer will they build houses and others live in them,
>> or plant and others eat.
> For as the days of a tree,
>> so will be the days of my people;
> my chosen ones will long enjoy
>> the work of their hands ...

Isaiah 65:19–22 (NIV UK)

Here we reflect on the industry of the past; and on all commerce that can provide for the wellbeing of all.

***

'Man's greatness is always to recreate his life, to recreate what is given to him, to fashion the very thing that he undergoes. Through work he produces his own natural existence. Through science he recreates the universe by means of symbols. Through art he recreates the alliance between his body and soul.'[3]

Simone Weil (1909–1943)

6. COLUMBA'S BAY

We are now moving to the south coast of the island. Columba's Bay is where, the legends say, the saint first came to shore with his twelve companions; from where he could no longer see his beloved Ireland; and where he buried his boat to prevent return.

> Grey eye there is
> that backward looks and gazes;
> never will it see again
> Ireland's women, Ireland's men.[4]

It is also likely, because he came among other Gaelic-speaking peoples, that he was granted an island that was already sacred. He returned several times to Ireland to further the work of developing monastic life, but Iona became his home. The poetry composed in his name, of exile from his own land and delight in the island, is a joy to us still, especially perhaps those homesick in a new land.

In Columba's society, to leave one's people for the love of God was considered a form of martyrdom. Exile was the worst sanction the law could impose upon a free man who had committed a heinous crime. Those who left for the love of God to go among strangers, where they had no kinsfolk to protect them and no status except what they earned, were like penitents, able to pray for their own betterment but also for those they left behind, even as they served as people of prayer in their new land.

***

This poem, in Latin *Noli Pater*, is attributed to Columba, and these lines could indeed date from his time:

> Father, do not allow thunder and lightning,
> lest we be shattered by its fear and its fire.
>
> We fear you, the terrible one, believing there is none like you.
> All songs praise you throughout the host of angels.
>
> Let the summits of heaven praise you, too,
> praise you with roaming lightning,
> O most loving Jesus, O righteous King of Kings.[5]

The first part of the bay is Port a'Churaich, Port of the Coracle, or Curragh. On the beach the green marble pebbles, smoothed by the sea and called locally 'Saint Columba's tears', can sometimes be found. The tradition in the past was that men working at sea would take one as a charm against drowning, echoing a pattern found among seafaring peoples the world over.

Today, people who make the pilgrimage on foot spend time at this bay to take two pebbles from this beach. One is to carry with them: a reminder of what they have received on Iona and wish to become part of their future.

The other is held while reflecting on what they no longer need or want to carry, but wish to leave behind without tainting other life. They throw this into the sea. We may do the same with one of the pebbles we brought from the shore before we entered the boat, reflecting for a moment in silence on what we wish to let go of, and then dropping this stone over the side, returning it to the sea. The other we may reflect on, and keep with us, to mark what we have received.

Pilgrims have always come here. High above the shoreline are great cairns of stones they created over the centuries. We can reflect on their heritage of faith, carried into the present.

Some years ago a stone labyrinth was laid out, and many people walk the winding routes, as people have done in certain holy places since the Middle Ages. They pause at the turns to reflect on the changes and winding of their own lives, as they travel the single route to the centre, and then by a second single entwined route outwards. While islanders clear away other labyrinths, which harm the common grazing, this one is left in place.

We may wish to sing here, something from our own repertoire, or the Wild Goose Resource Group song 'Come, bring your burdens to God' (from *We Walk His Way*, Wild Goose Publications).

We pass the jutting headland shaped like a boat, with the small islands to the south, past the second part of Saint Columba's Bay, called the 'Port of the False Man', and along the rocky coast under the hill on which the highest point is called the 'Cairn of the Back to Ireland'. Here Columba is said to have looked back to make sure that his native land was not visible, and then settled on Iona.

Inland from here, at the head of the valley that runs down to Saint Columba's Bay, is Loch Staonaig. Its soft, peaty water was the source for the island after the end of the use of wells in the village, and into the 1990s.

We can pray here for the work of women, which is often overlooked but essential. The southern part of the island once belonged to the nuns of Iona, and for centuries after their time the valley leading down to Saint Columba's Bay was associated with the work of women.

It was used as summer pasture for cattle, a place where they were milked, and butter and cheese made for winter sustenance. The geological complexity of this small island gives it these small areas of fertility and shelter. Those who recorded Iona during the medieval periods and then in the sixteenth, seventeenth and eighteenth centuries remark on the island's relative fertility, and the growing of barley for beer.

Crofting, combined with fishing, has long been the main way of life in these islands. This involved small-scale growing of food for the home, dairying and sheep husbandry, often on common grazing, to provide the wool for homespun clothing, leather and meat for times of celebration.

> 'Very truly I tell you, unless a grain of wheat falls to the ground and dies, it remains only a single seed. But if it dies, it produces many seeds.'
>
> John 12:24 (NIV UK)

> Lord, you have been our dwelling place
>   throughout all generations.
> Before the mountains were born
>   or you brought forth the whole world,
>   from everlasting to everlasting you are God.
>
> You turn people back to dust,
>   saying, 'Return to dust, you mortals.'
> A thousand years in your sight
>   are like a day that has just gone by,
>   or like a watch in the night.

Yet you sweep people away in the sleep of death –
    they are like the new grass of the morning:
In the morning it springs up new,
    but by evening it is dry and withered …

Our days may come to seventy years,
    or eighty, if our strength endures …

May the favour of the Lord our God rest on us;
    establish the work of our hands for us –
    yes, establish the work of our hands.

Psalm 90:1–6,10a, 17 (NIV UK)

We pray for those who work in agriculture, and that the love of the land that feeds us may continue. We reflect on modern methods of large-scale production for anonymous customers, and the damage it permits. We pray for the way of life in these islands, and that the skills of growing food in a way that does no damage may never be rebuffed, nor may we ever take too much. That we may form a world where all have enough to eat.

7. THE BOILING POT

As we round the south-west corner of Iona, we come to a place where it is always windy. These narrow straits between Iona and an offshore rocky islet are known as the Boiling Pot. The journey here may be too rough for other than personal reflection on the places of anger in our own lives, those destructive and those productive, those on private and those on public matters, and how, here in our pilgrimage, we seek to assimilate both into our lives.

8. BAY AT THE BACK OF THE OCEAN

We continue past the Spouting Cave, and then on to the largest bay and the machair, where the walking pilgrimage path from Loch Staonaig comes down to the shore.

This bay, *Camus Cùl an Taibh*, is the widest on Iona. To the west is the Isle of Tiree, the 'low island of barley' where Iona's monks had many interests; and the more rugged Isle of Coll is to its north. The stories about Saint Columba often emphasise the dangers of sea voyage, even to these nearby islands.

A ship, the *Guy Mannering*, was wrecked here in the nineteenth century, with some loss of life. The obelisk in the Reilig Odhràin cemetery to the south of the chapel is a memorial to those from the *Guy Mannering* buried there. Sometimes lumps of coal from this ship are still washed ashore.

We now move from the work of the sea to the work of the land.

9. THE MACHAIR

The Gaelic word *machair*, meaning light, sandy land of a raised beach, with a high seashell content, and with a particular plant-life, has become a scientific term. Like many Hebridean islands, Iona has a west coast machair, which has long been used communally for agriculture. The lighter soils are free of the peatiness of much of the island, making machair easy to work, and the drainage and lower acidic content allowing crops to grow well. The Iona machair was worked at least by the time of Adomnán in the seventh century and very probably from the time of Columba a hundred years earlier. It was used for growing crops as recently as the Second World War, and the outlines can still be seen of the strips, rigs, running seawards. Now grazed by sheep and used by golfers, the walking pilgrimage stops here for a time, so people can share their lunch and stories.

Looking landwards to the gate where the island's road ends, we can see on the right a distinctive low hill. In recent times this has often been known as the Hill of the Fairies, but has sometimes been equated with the hill mentioned in Adomnán's *Life of Saint Columba*, on which Columba was seen conversing with angels, and so is also known as the Hill of the Angels. Angels are the heavenly messengers often associated with mystical experience, mentioned in many cultures.

> I know a man in Christ who fourteen years ago was caught up to the third heaven. Whether it was in the body or out of the body I do not know – God knows. And I know that this man – whether in the body or apart from the body I do not know, but God knows – was caught up to paradise

and heard inexpressible things, things that no one is permitted to tell.

2 Corinthians 12:2–4 (NIV UK)

The machair is a place to reflect on our climate, on the flowers we find here, which are mostly small and seemingly insignificant but are vital to insects that pollinate and uphold our world's fragile ecosystem.

Here we may reflect also on travel, on the dangers of crossing the seas. The machair is also a place to reflect on our last, abiding home; and the 'angelic messengers' which that home sends to us through our fellow-humans, through the world around us, or by other means.

***

Bless to me, O God,
The earth beneath my foot.
Bless to me, O God,
The path whereon I go;
Bless to me, O God,
The thing of my desire;
Thou Evermore of evermore.
Bless Thou to me my rest.

Bless to me the thing
Whereon is set my mind,
Bless to me the thing
Whereon is set my love;

Bless to me the thing
Whereon is set my hope;
O Thou King of kings,
Bless Thou to me mine eye! [6]

From Carmina Gadelica

10. ALONG THE COAST

As we move northwards (or southwards if we are travelling anti-clockwise round the island), just past the machair and the little Port Bàn, the White Port, named on account of its sand, we see inland a small hill known as Dùn Bhuirg, the Hill of the Fort. This is an ancient viewpoint for overseeing arrivals from the west, and provided a place of protection for animals and people, from the elements and from unwelcome visitors. They were not the first, for before farmers there were people here: a Mesolithic shell-midden has even been found on the island from the time when our ancestors were nomadic hunter-gatherers of the coastlines.

We pass under the island's highest point, Dùn Ì, with the cairn composed of stones placed there by those who climb the hill. Near the summit is a natural spring, named 'Well of Eternal Youth'. Below it, inland and out of sight, is the 'Hermit's Cell', a circular ruin of stones which may date back to the time of the Columban monastery, or may be older still. Nearby, under a small cliff, is an enclosure for animals, and also nearby is another source of fresh water called the 'Well of the North Wind'.

Mar tobar glé trí croí na lice, brúchtann an dóchas trí croí an dhuine.

Like a clear spring through the heart of a stone, hope breaks out through the human heart.

Irish folk proverb

Hermit

He stayed amongst bare stones
of ancient shelter at the centre
of sanctuary, with birds, beetles, bracken to sweeten
the Way when the dry well within
bored in darkness.
Did grey Novembers
sourced from remembered springs,
past tales, brothers' plaints, let
rare bursts of living water
pour stars in the heart?

Rosemary Power

11. THE NORTH COAST

As we follow the rocky coastline, we have another reminder of the past, for pieces of limestone still wash ashore from the hold of a sailing ship once wrecked here. As we turn around the end of the coastline, we see the sands where people come to walk, play, swim and rest. In the early days of the Iona Community people camped here.

First we pass Eilean Chalbha, Iona's little 'calf' of an island, and see many of the larger islands on a good day: the now-uninhabited Treshnish Islands with the distinctive shape of Dutchman's Cap; Staffa, where Fingal's Cave was celebrated by Felix Mendelssohn in his *Hebridean Overture*; Ulva and Gometra under the mountainous coast of west Mull; and many smaller islands.

Thus the heavens and the earth were completed in all their vast array.

By the seventh day God had finished the work he had been doing; so on the seventh day he rested from all his work. Then God blessed the seventh day and made it holy, because on it he rested from all the work of creating that he had done.

Genesis 2:1–3 (NIV UK)

In Alistair Maclean's book *Hebridean Altars* he speaks of an old man from Mull who says that God created the Hebrides on the eighth day:

The world was finished and the Good One was mighty

tired and took a rest and, while He was resting He thought: 'Well, I have let my earth-children see the power of my mind, in rock and mountain and tree and wind and flower. And I have shown them the likeness of my mind, for I have made theirs like my own. And I have shown them the love of my mind, for I have made them happy. But halt,' says the Good One to himself, 'I have not shown them the beauty of my mind.' So the next day, and that was the eighth day, he takes up a handful of jewels and opens a window in the sky and throws them down into the sea. And those jewels are the Hebrides.[7]

We reflect on the gift of beauty, for this land in rain, wind and sunshine. For the gift of rest, the recreative time that allows us enjoyment, and our minds' recovery. For those who are trapped in places without beauty, neither in the natural world nor in the minds and actions of the people with whom they are surrounded. One day may they find views like this opening to them, and be glad.

We pray that we may become better stewards, of our world and of each other; that future generations may find ways to repair what we have taken from them, that they too may rest after their work, and play.

***

The Spirit's coming

> Not with a roll of drums
> > nor trumpet's blare
> but clothed in silence comes
> > love down the stair.
>
> After the flames' quick roar,
> > the whirlwind storm,
> with still and stronger core
> > love fills our form.
>
> Then in the noise and spin
> > of our small days,
> quiet amid the din,
> > love moulds our ways.

Margaret Connor [8]

Right at the north end of the island is another echo of the past use of the land, for fresh water comes out of the sand in one place, and was used to wash the flax that was grown for linen-making.

12. WHITE STRAND OF THE MONKS

As we turn eastwards into the Sound of Iona, we come upon another long stretch of golden sand. This is associated with the monks of the abbey. In peaceful times they may have come here to gather the fruits of the seashore for their diet, seaweeds for food and fertiliser, and shellfish to make the coloured dyes that decorated their manuscripts.

But it is also associated with the arrival between the late eighth and the eleventh centuries of the Vikings, who beached their ships and floated them off at high tide.

Vikings had no understanding of, and so no respect for, the sacred boundaries of ditch and dyke, within which was sanctuary under the protection of Saint Columba. They came to loot, to capture young men and women as slaves to sell on to unknown futures; and sometimes in the heat of the attack, they burnt the place they raided. Iona suffered several times.

Over time, the raiders were replaced by settlers from Scandinavia, and they turned to Christianity. Some were buried in the abbey precincts. Later, their written accounts call Iona *'ey in helga'*, 'the holy island', and though sporadic raiding still continued, the newcomers intermarried, and became part of Hebridean life.

The White Strand of the Monks is a place of blessing beneath and beyond all that has happened. Wisdom, *Anima*, *Ruach*, the breath of the Spirit, is present here in wind, waves, healing and history.

> 'The LORD brought me forth as the first of his works,
>   before his deeds of old;

I was formed long ages ago,
    at the very beginning, when the world came to be.
When there were no watery depths, I was given birth,
    when there were no springs overflowing with water;
before the mountains were settled in place,
    before the hills, I was given birth,
before he made the world or its fields
    or any of the dust of the earth.
I was there when he set the heavens in place,
    when he marked out the horizon on the face of the deep,
when he established the clouds above
    and fixed securely the fountains of the deep,
when he gave the sea its boundary
    so that the waters would not overstep his command,
and when he marked out the foundations of the earth.
    Then I was constantly at his side.
I was filled with delight day after day,
    rejoicing always in his presence,
rejoicing in his whole world
    and delighting in the human race …'

Proverbs 8:22–31 (NIV UK)

We reflect, in this place of peace today, on the suffering and violence in the world, on the focus on self and our own survival that lets us take what others need. We recall that we have received benefits in these islands through our ancestors' financial and other gain, from, among other sources, what was once the transatlantic slave trade. We may consider the easy ways in which we can treat certain people as less in value, feeling and ability than ourselves.

We reflect on the true gift of our skills and their place in the lives of our neighbours. And on those moments when we feel the arms of God holding all creation.

**

A day of grace

The time is right;
      a day of grace
may lead us to the hidden place
as dawn shakes off the drab of night
revealing now a fleeting sight
of something far beyond our base
material needs. It is the face
of heaven, if we know it right
and hope to comprehend that light.

The time is right
but we do not control the pace
on journeys out of time and space.
Our human efforts are too slight,
our aims ephemeral, yet we might
still hope to grasp
      a day of grace:
the time is right.

Margaret Connor

13. TOWARDS THE ABBEY

As we turn back into the Sound of Iona we see the abbey from a different angle. It sits in a managed landscape. Once the land would have been covered with trees or scrub. Its current bare features have much to do with sheep-grazing, and remind us that much of the landscape of the Islands was created in the last two and a half centuries, when the people were displaced and forced overseas, to make way for the sheep that landowners deemed more profitable.

A shallow loch above the MacLeod Centre and under Dùn Ì was drained in the eighteenth century to make use of the peat it provided, a process that made the once-strong millstream into a small burn, which still runs by the gate of the MacLeod Centre and down to the sea just north of the abbey buildings.

The staff at the centres come from across the world to work on behalf of the Iona Community. Guests too have come from every walk of life. People come, perhaps attending a service after many years of avoiding them, or never having been in a church, or worn out by church, or wearied by grief, or seeking to renew their joy in faith, or searching for something unnameable.

> The apostles gathered round Jesus and reported to him all they had done and taught. Then, because so many people were coming and going that they did not even have a chance to eat, he said to them, 'Come with me by yourselves to a quiet place and get some rest.'
>
> So they went away by themselves in a boat to a solitary place.
>
> *Mark 6:30–33 (NIV UK)*

We reflect on the world we have received from the past, the contributions to this island; the work received from people from every continent; and the international network of love that binds us together. We ask guidance for the future of the Church as God wishes it.

***

We bless you, O God, for that church at home.
Let us remember its frailties.
It is often too frail for the modern storm,
is that church at home.
Too conformist to a world that's dying.
Too respectable for the drunkard
or the wretch to feel at home.
Too keen about its money to accuse an acquisitive society.
Too concerned about its own internal peace
to say the scarifying word about the Cross
as the way of peace for the world …

And just because each one of us is that church at home,
help us to view again
our attitude to money in the light of your poverty,
our attitude to drunkards and the lecherous
in the light of your love for them,
our attitude to war
in the light of your strange way of dealing with it.

Lest, when we speak so critically
of the frailty of our church at home,

in our walks we should confront you, Lord Christ,
suddenly at the bend of the road
and not escape your silent gaze at us,
your silent gaze at each one of us
so clearly saying:

'You are the cause of the frailty of the church at home.'

George MacLeod [9]

14. HEADING SOUTHWARDS

There is a story that after the Reformation hundreds of crosses on Iona were torn down and thrown into the sea. In the late 1950s, these were actually searched for in the sea below the abbey, but nothing was found. Aptly though, the divers' boat was named *Calum Cille*.

South of the abbey is the Reilig Odhràin Chapel, the only surviving building from the Columban monastery, raised in the twelfth century. It is an important place to many who come here on pilgrimage, for its powerful atmosphere of prayer, for the birds that nest in its rafters, and for the beautiful echoing sound of music when played here. (See pages 29–35.)

The cemetery that surrounds it is the place of rest for modern islanders as well as the kings and warriors of earlier times. Below this chapel and the ruins of Saint Mary's Chapel in the field below it, just north of Bishop's House, the Episcopalian Retreat Centre, is the little Port na Muintir, Port of the Community. This was traditionally the landing place of the monks, and south of it under the Argyll Hotel is the small Port Adomnàn, which once had a high cross standing above it, and is named after the Abbot of Iona who wrote the *Life of Saint Columba*. Port Adomnàn joins Saint Ronan's Bay as we return to the jetty, and beyond the houses of the village are the ruins of the nunnery.

15. THE NUNNERY AND THE RETURN

We see the nunnery ruins coming into view behind the village. We do not know when there was first a community of religious women on Iona, and recent research suggests that there may have been one before the Viking Age. This medieval nunnery was raised in the late twelfth century (see pages 36–45). Although the numbers who lived here were not high, the rhythm of prayer, study and practical work went on during most of its history. The community probably had a hostel for women pilgrims. Eventually, after the Reformation, the remaining handful of elderly nuns handed over the buildings to others. Their cemetery continued as a burial ground for women and young children.

> When the LORD restored the fortunes of Zion,
>   we were like those who dreamed.
> Our mouths were filled with laughter,
>   our tongues with songs of joy.
> Then it was said among the nations,
>   'The LORD has done great things for them.'
> The LORD has done great things for us,
>   and we are filled with joy.
> Restore our fortunes, LORD,
>   like streams in the Negev.

> Those who sow with tears
>   will reap with songs of joy.
> Those who go out weeping,
>   carrying seed to sow,
> will return with songs of joy,
>   carrying sheaves with them.

Psalm 126 (NIV UK)

We recall the lives of the largely unknown women who prayed here for centuries. We remember those women who have been resident on this island, in hard times and good, those forced by poverty or drawn by adventure to leave.

***

'Pure inspiration', we may claim and smile,
    not thinking that perhaps another sphere
        might spur the ones who go the second mile
            and cheer our working scene when they are near.

Long since the age of apostolic fire
    and in the pressure of a crowded day,
        when best laid plans will go no higher,
            we yet may catch a spark along the way.

And sometimes, in a most unlikely place,
    a sign, it seems, will surface in the fray
        to filter through a stranger's friendly face
            and shed a light along our path today.

Margaret Connor

16. BACK TO THE JETTY

We reflect on the journey, the arriving, the waiting and the leaving. We and others will leave from this point into our unknown future. Meanwhile, as pilgrims and strangers on this earth, seeking our eternal home, we give thanks for the people of the island today, for boatmen and ferry crew, for all who work here and live here.

***

Never weather-beaten sail more willing bent to shore,
Never tired pilgrim's limbs affected slumber more,
Than my wearied sprite now longs to fly out of my
troubled breast:
   O come quickly, sweetest Lord, and take my soul to rest.

Ever-blooming are the joys of Heaven's high paradise,
Cold age deafs not there our ears, nor vapour dims our eyes:
Glory there the Sun outshines, whose beams the blessed
only see;
   O come quickly, glorious Lord, and raise my sprite to thee.

Thomas Campion (1567–1620)

'sprite' – spirit

AFTERWORD

Pilgrimage is a state of mind, and of heart. The urge to explore, to do so while passing through places of beauty, in a group, alone but meeting others on the way, or entirely alone in the twentieth-century manner, is an ancient route to the heart of things.

Walking brings the blood to the front of the brain, creativity and the imagination are stimulated, and people engage with encounters that are out of the normal routine of their lives. Coming to Iona opens people up because this is a place where people have prayed deeply and left an imprint on the atmosphere that many if not most people feel.

Walking to a specific place has become increasingly part of life for many people, and while a medieval pilgrim to Iona or Compostela or further afield would expect to be away for some years, or might die on the way, a modern pilgrim might fit their activity into their annual leave. Or, for those without the financial support of a job behind them, the walking may need to be local or be undertaken in the mind. The traditional aspect of setting one's material affairs in order beforehand is now rarely a direct part of the preparation, nor is expiation of sin and hope of an easeful death part of the purpose. But the desire to explore, and to encounter a deeper reason for life, is present for most, even if they are not intentionally searching for a deeper connection with God. For some it may simply be that a walking route with places of interest is the starting point. This is not new: pilgrimage was to many of our forebears a version of the package holiday.

For those who cannot make the physical journey, some of these aspects may be worth bearing in mind imaginatively. Pilgrimage once put the body on the line through hardships and the dangers of an unknown landscape with its physical perils, and the different perils of wild animals and other human beings. Nowadays, with modern technology and communications, most of the journeys may be less hazardous. However, for people with limited mobility the body may be on the line in another way, which requires equal courage to rise to a daily challenge. There is also the pilgrimage of the mind. On Iona we have the chance to enter into stillness through our experience of the natural world, and also enter stillness through the creative artistry of others. We touch the lives of those who have made their lives here over the centuries, and have left something of their story in the stones.

Prayer is a creative act that engages with the Creator. As with all creativity it is creative even when it seems that nothing is happening and only perseverance is required. Prayer is also, for many people, made concrete by the enjoyment of art, poetry, music, and other means; and for some this sparks their own creativity.

The prayer and poetry included in this book is there to be used as far as it is relevant or useful to the reader, but then replaced by their own expressions of the experience of this island. We pray, in this place where unity with the divine is easier than in the routine of daily life, where the stones cry out when we forget to unite with the Creator, for the healing of the nations, and the healing of the individual soul.

As well as our own inner life, there is a wider world to which prayer unites the individual and where healing is equally needed. Seeking to unite with God through contemplation results in practical consequences that in turn assist our growth.

We have experienced the Covid-19 pandemic, a final warning that, as climate changes and our attitudes and disregard for the costs remain unchanged, we will face further pandemics, massive movements of people as their own homes become unbearable, the economic crises that go with such change, and increasing warfare as basics like shelter, food and water become in yet shorter supply. Pilgrimage and its opportunities for reflection, and sometimes discussion, helps us to change as we make choices that may be costly but are ultimately joy-filled, that take us away from a consumer society with its offer of a locked-away half-life, and through crying out for justice for others, and acting for justice, allow us to be contributors to the goodness of the world.

Iona is a place where changes happen. May our pilgrimage here tread lightly, and may we leave nothing behind but the power of our prayer to change the world.

Glen Nant

That day before spring
the westering sun touched
brown boughs pale gold
and birch trunks glowed
soft silver.

Did once tired feet
seeking elusive Love
come down the glen and see
the pilgrim path alight with hint
of hope beyond their time?

Did the Nant wash
stained bruises, soil, off soles,
and Cruachan raise her crown,
white still and wheeled
with eagles, her flanks
sheltering deer?

Did the sun touch
plague-weary wanderers
of our time, rootless and yearning
for lands behind the light?

Was each enclosed in glow that day
embracing hungry body and defeated mind,
and shine pale gold?

Rosemary Power, March 2021

Glen Nant, near Taynuilt, Argyll, is part of a medieval pilgrimage route.

SOURCES

Part one – Places of prayer

1. 'Border presentation', by Rosemary Power, first published in *Beyond Brexit: Prayers at a Time of Division*, Rosemary Power (Ed.), Wild Goose Publications, 2019

2. 'O King of Friday' translated from Diarmuid Ó Laoghaire, ed. and trans., *Ár bPaidreacha Dúchais, Baile Átha Cliath: Foilseacháin Ábhair Spioradálta*, 1982, no. 301, p.102

3. *If This Is a Woman: Inside Ravensbrück: Hitler's Concentration Camp for Women*, Little, Brown, 2015

Part two – A cloister pilgrimage

1. *Carmina Gadelica: Hymns and Incantations*, Alexander Carmichael, Floris Books, 1992, no.14, p.45 (shortened)

2. 'The grace of the Spirit be with us ...' Translation based on the Irish in *Abhráin Diadha Chúige Connacht*, or *The Religious Songs of Connacht: A Collection of Poems, Stories, Prayers, Satires, Ranns, Charms, etc.*, Douglas Hyde (Dubhghlas de hÍde), T. Fisher Unwin, M.H. Gill & Son Ltd., 1906, rep. 1972, Irish University Press, ii, p.78

3. Edwin Muir, from 'One Foot in Eden', from *Edwin Muir: Collected Poems*, Faber and Faber, 1979

4. From *Households of God: Rule of St Benedict, with Explanations for Monks and Lay-people Today*, David Parry, Darton, Longman & Todd Ltd, 1980

5. From 'God's grandeur', by Gerard Manley Hopkins, written in 1877, published in 1918

6. *Carmina Gadelica: Hymns and Incantations*, Alexander Carmichael, Floris Books, 1992, p.368, no. 402

7. *Carmina Gadelica: Hymns and Incantations*, Alexander Carmichael, Floris Books, 1992, p.371, no. 408

8. 'After the ceasefire', by Rosemary Power, first published in *Coracle: the magazine of the Iona Community*, autumn 2014

9. Based on Diarmuid Ó Laoghaire, ed. and trans., *Ár bPaidreacha Dúchais, Baile Átha Cliath: Foilseacháin Ábhair Spioradálta*, 1982, no. 214, pp.69-70. Translated prayer originally published in *Timíre*, 1928

10. From *A Celtic Miscellany*, selected and translated by Kenneth Hurlstone Jackson, Penguin Classics, 1970, p.136

Part three – Pilgrimage by boat

1. Thomas Merton, from *Thoughts in Solitude*, Thomas Merton

2. 'Bread broken', by Kate McIlhagga, from *Encompassing Presence: Prayer Handbook 1993*, United Reformed Church, 1993. A revised version is found in *The Green Heart of the Snowdrop*, Kate McIlhagga, Wild Goose Publications, 2004

3. Simone Weil, from 'The Mysticism of Work', in *Simone Weil: An Anthology*, Siân Miles (Ed.), Virago Press, 1986, p.178

4. Translation by James Carney, from *Medieval Irish Lyrics with The Irish Bardic Poet*, Dolmen Press, 1985, p.87

5. Translated by Thomas Owen Clancy and Gilbert Márkus, from *Iona: The Earliest Poetry of a Celtic Monastery*, p.85. Used with permission

6. *Carmina Gadelica: Hymns and Incantations*, Alexander Carmichael, Floris Books, 1992, no. 244

7. From *Hebridean Altars: The Spirit of an Island Race*, Alistair Maclean, Moray Press, 1937

8. Poems by Margaret Connor used by permission

9. From *The Whole Earth Shall Cry Glory: Iona Prayers*, Wild Goose Publications, 2006

Bible passages from: Holy Bible, New International Version®, NIV® Copyright ©1973, 1978, 1984, 2011 by Biblica, Inc.® Used by permission. All rights reserved worldwide.

Photo credits:

Reilig Odhràin door, p.29; Nunnery side-chapel arch, p.36; Nunnery arcade, p.42; Holy Island quernstone, p.51; *Descent of the Spirit*, p.53, and Open book, p.62, by Rosemary Power. All other photos by David Coleman

FURTHER READING

'A New Jerusalem "at the ends of the Earth": Interpreting Charles Thomas's Excavations at Iona Abbey', 1956-63, E. Campbell and A. Maldonado, *Antiquaries Journal*, 2020, 1-53. Open Access article, Creative Commons Attribution

A Pilgrim's Guide to Iona Abbey, Chris Polhill, Wild Goose Publications, 2006

An Iona Anthology, Marian McNeill, second edition, Iona Community, 1952, New Iona Press, 1990

Around a Thin Place: An Iona Pilgrimage Guide, Jane Bentley and Neil Paynter, Wild Goose Publications, 2011

Churches in Early Medieval Ireland: Architecture, Ritual and Memory, Tomás Ó Carragáin, Yale University Press, 2010

Columba's Island, Iona from Past to Present, E. Mairi MacArthur, Edinburgh University Press, 1995, revised 2007

'Dating Iona's Nunnery', Rosemary Power, *Scottish Historical Review* 253, 2021, 277-284

Early Irish Lyrics, Gerard Murphy, Oxford University Press, 1956, reprinted Four Courts Press, 1999

Excavations in Iona 1964 to 1974, Richard Reece, 1981

Flowers of Iona: A Botanical Guide, Jean M. Millar, The Iona Community, 1972, fifth edition, Isle of Iona Press, 2019

Iona Abbey and Nunnery, Peter Yeoman and Nicki Scott, Historic Environment Scotland, 2020

Iona: A Map, by Diarmid (revised and updated version), Wild Goose Publications

Iona, Colin Baxter Guides, Colin Baxter Photography, 1997, 2001

Iona, Fiona Macleod (William Sharp), 1910. Usually published with *The Divine Adventure*

'Iona's Sheela-na-gig and Its Visual Context', Rosemary Power, *Folklore* 123, 2012, 330-54

Image and Vision: Reflecting with the Book of Kells, Rosemary Power, Veritas, 2021

Life of Saint Columba, Adomnán, edited and translated by Richard Sharp, Penguin Books, 1991

Martyrology of Oengus the Culdee, Óengus mac Óengobann, Whitley Stokes, 1905, reprinted 1984. https://celt.ucc.ie/published/G200001.html

Peter Abelard, Helen Waddell, Constable, 1933

The Cloisters of Iona Abbey, Ewan Mathers, Wild Goose Publications, 2001

The Deer's Cry: A Treasury of Irish Religious Verse, Patrick Murray (Ed), Four Courts Press, 1986

That Illustrious Island ... Iona through Travellers' Eyes, E. Mairi MacArthur, New Iona Press, 1991

'The poetry of Ailean Dall', Ronald Black, in *Gael and Lowlander in Scottish Literature: Cross-currents in Scottish Writing in the Nineteenth Century*, Christopher MacLachlan and Ronald W. Renton (Eds), Association for Scottish Literary Studies, 2015

The Story of Iona: An Illustrated History and Guide, Rosemary Power, Canterbury Press, 2012

The Triumph Tree: Scotland's Earliest Poetry, Thomas Clancy (Ed.), Canongate, 1998

Vickery's Folk Flora: An A-Z of the Folklore and Uses of British and Irish Plants, Roy Vickery, W&N, 2019

Wild Flowers of Iona: Some of the More Common Varieties, Joyce Watson, Iona (privately printed), 2019

Wild Goose Publications, the publishing house of the Iona Community established in the Celtic Christian tradition of Saint Columba, produces books, e-books, CDs and digital downloads on:

- holistic spirituality
- social justice
- political and peace issues
- healing
- innovative approaches to worship
- song in worship, including the work of the Wild Goose Resource Group
- material for meditation and reflection

Visit our website at
www.ionabooks.com
for details of all our products and online sales

Printed in Great Britain
by Amazon

"You have played an important role in supporting the work of HMP Springhill towards Enabling Environment Accreditation, building the culture required to sustain this and demonstrating our shared commitment. The assessment day was a really inspiring session to be involved in. I offer you my personal thanks for your contribution." HMP Governor

"I really love the guide to creating a rehabilitative culture you've created. This is brilliantly and imaginatively presented, using the alphabet, with entries from A to Z and in your usual accessible style. I have distributed this to the National Rehabilitative Culture Team to be used as a resource for staff induction. I am so grateful to you for your work on this document and really appreciate your generosity with your talents." HMP Governor

"Philip Martin spoke at HMP Brixton about rehabilitation. The event was attended by representatives from 5 London jails including Governors and Operational Staff. His presentation was excellent and his content inspirational; he spoke about his experiences of rehabilitative culture and how staff can have had a big impact on the people in their care. He also produced quality hand-outs for all of the attendees to take away. Overall, the day was a big success." HMP Custodial Manager

Thank you for purchasing and reading this book, please be kind enough to leave a review, which will be really appreciated.

You can also tweet @philmartinuk or contact me via www.PhilMartin.co.uk